QUALITY
CONTROLLED

Personal Fulfillment Through
Professional Organization

Quality Controlled - Personal Fulfillment Through Professional Organization
Copyright © 2018 Ryan B. Greene

Greene Publishing

Book design by:
Arbor Services, Inc.
www.arborservices.co/

Printed in the United States of America

Quality Controlled - Personal Fulfillment Through Professional Organization
Ryan B. Greene

1. Title 2. Author 3. Self-Help

Library of Congress Control Number: 2017915206
ISBN 13: 978-0-692-96033-2

QUALITY
CONTROLLED

Personal Fulfillment Through
Professional Organization

RYAN B. GREENE

Greene Publishing

This book is dedicated to

my wife Lindsey, you are my rock. Thank you for always supporting my crazy dreams and ideas. This dream came true in print form. To my son Karsen, chase your dreams with everything you have and know that I will always be there to support you. To my daughter Kynlee, never stop smiling! You surprise me everyday with your kindness and laughter, I am so proud to be your dad.

To my Dad, Mom, Brothers Brad and Dusty, thank you all for the growing moments in my life. I would not be the person I am today without all of you and for that I am truly grateful.

To the readers, thank you for taking the time to read this book, I hope this book changes your life for the better!

Contents

Introduction

Is it possible to have too much of a good thing? By definition, the fact that the "thing" is "good" implies that the answer would be no. But nearly everything can be enjoyed to excess, and when in excess, the "goodness" factor can quickly evaporate. Consider how the pursuit of excessive wealth can lead to neglecting loved ones, and overindulging in food inevitably causes poor health. Even exercise, taken to an extreme, can cause exhaustion and physical injury.

On a global scale, abundance has led to scarcity of resources, pollution, climate change, and other problems. Clearly, too much of a good thing can lead us down an undesirable path.

Let's face it . . . we live in a culture that values excess and quantity. More is typically seen as better. Keeping up with the Joneses usually means having the same size home and number of toys as our neighbors. Whether it's our homes, our cars, or our fashion, we tend to pursue quantity over quality. But is this really what we want or need? Wouldn't you rather have a high-quality lifestyle rather than one immersed in abundance? If so, then how can we make decisions and choices that consistently promote quality over quantity?

My pursuit of quantity began relatively early in life. Since the age of fifteen years, I have worked in the family business, an energy services company. What began as a summer job performing some of the more physically demanding tasks soon evolved into holding every foreseeable position in the growing company. From welder to welding inspector to operations supervisor to quality control manager, I have performed nearly every duty required to make the business run smoothly. The more skills I acquired, the more marketable and happy I thought I would be, but I found this to not always be the case.

While working at my family's business, I also began pursuing other personal entrepreneurial interests. My motivation, at least in part, was to attain independent financial success, but unfortunately, each of my ventures proved to be unsuccessful in achieving this goal. I tended to judge my efforts based on the bottom line in the accounting ledger, and therefore, I invariably concluded that my time had been wasted. Certainly, the goal of any business is to earn a profit. Without question, a business won't be in business long without it. But to say these ventures were complete failures would be rather short sighted.

My personal revelation that quality of life was more important than the quantity of accomplishments and acquisitions happened rather fortuitously. After our company's quality control manager suddenly became ill with a protracted condition, I assumed his responsibilities. I had some idea about what quality control meant, and like most every other task I had undertaken, I sought to learn as much as I could as quickly as possible. I learned quality control processes like the 5 Ps, total quality management, strategic quality management, and Six Sigma. Before I knew it, I had mastered the techniques to ensure better production and services.

Had I simply mastered this skill set like I had done with so many others previously, that might be the end of the story. But as I applied these quality control measures to our business, I realized that these same techniques could be applied to my own career pursuits. In fact, they could be applied in every aspect of my personal life. Was I seeking to attain the standards I defined as important in my job and career? In my relationships? In my pursuit of good health? Was the time I allocated to each of these areas quality time and prioritized according to what I valued? And if not, how could I change my behaviors to better align my goals with my actions?

As I considered these questions, I also realized that my past "failures" in business had not truly been failures at all. Each experience had added tremendous value to my life. With every failure came new insight and knowledge, providing me with a deeper perspective on what it was I actually wanted. These failures, if that's what society calls them, were some of my greatest teachers . . . not only about the rights and wrongs of business, but about who I was and wanted to be. Though they had not been well aligned with the pursuit of a more quality-focused life, they had been beneficial as a guide for change.

From these experiences, I realized my inner passions stemmed from a continual need to expand and grow. This desire explained why I had held so many positions in the family company as well as my constant experimentation with other businesses. My burning desire to learn has led me down many paths. From certifications in leadership, life coaching, and mentoring, to advanced training in speaking and psychology, I have continued to grow and develop in my understanding of human nature and human desires. These activities add quality to my life as they fulfill a deep, inner need for me personally.

With these new insights into myself, and with a growing knowledge of quality control, the idea of applying quality control principles to my personal life was born. The first question I asked myself was whether my own level of expectations in my life's pursuits had been filled. While I was satisfied and content in many ways, my expectations were certainly not completely met. Armed with this new truth, the next question followed quite naturally. What exactly were my ideal standards in life . . . in my career, my relationships, my spending habits? And what would it take for me to meet these standards?

Through this process, I have literally turned my life around. I no longer feel like I am simply tackling more and more projects and tasks to pad my resume or enrich my skill sets. Instead, I have a purpose. I know what I need for a quality-filled life, and I have defined these standards and expectations accordingly. In doing so, I have created a yardstick by which I can assess every area of my life.

And if things are moving in the wrong direction, I have a process in place that allows me to quickly get back on track. I call this the Quality Core Process, and by using it, you can have the quality life you desire as well.

Perhaps like me, you have read dozens of self-help books and pursued many courses and seminars related to self-improvement. While many offer good advice, I almost always walked away feeling less than satisfied. I was still pursuing quantity over quality. I did not have a practical guide to define, assess, and change my own personal behaviors that would lead me toward a higher-quality life. However, once I started applying quality control principles to my personal life, this all changed. I realized that I was in complete control and that I could be happy and fulfilled by shifting my pursuits toward quality rather than quantity.

The Quality Core Process differs from other self-help manuals in a number of ways. It allows both for standards and personalized strategies tailored to you for achieving a quality life. And it can be applied to one area of your life or many. The process, once you grasp it, can be applied to any aspect of your life. The Quality Core Process is both consistent and dynamic enough to serve as your guide to a better and more fulfilling life. More is not always better . . . unless it leads to a life that is truly quality focused.

SECTION 1:

The Basics of Quality Core

Chapter 1

What Is Quality Core?

More than two-thirds of Americans are reported to be either unhappy or dissatisfied with their current jobs or careers. Many believe the American dream is something that is no longer attainable. And overall enjoyment in life, as measured by certain indices like the Happiness Index, suggest only a third of Americans are very happy.[1] In a country of such wealth, opportunity, and abundance, why are these statistics so low? And with these findings, what are Americans doing to change their situation?

A single reason will not explain these phenomena or identify the different approaches people are taking to resolve their dilemmas. However, one common theme does appear to underlie these findings. Despite most of our basic needs being met (even to excess in many instances), something remains lacking. According to Abraham Maslow, our higher-level needs are being unfulfilled . . . intimacy, achievement, and our perceived potential. Unlike basic needs like

1Harris Poll, "Latest Happiness Index reveals American happiness at all-time low," HarrisPoll.com, 2016, http://www.theharrispoll.com/health-and-life/American-Happiness-at-All-Time-Low.html.

food, clothing, shelter, and protection, these higher-level needs require a focus on quality over quantity. And it is here we will begin our conversation about quality core.

Quality Versus Quantity

It's an age-old debate. Is it better to have more of an inferior item or experience or to have less of a superior one? I could choose to have three cups of Maxwell House coffee to jump-start my Monday morning or a single cup of my premium roast from Starbucks. I can invest in a set of Bose wireless headphones, or I could go through half a dozen pairs of cheap wired headphones from the neighborhood convenience store. Each of us makes these quality and quantity decisions in our lives every day with little thought about their importance.

Are these decisions important? If I get my morning dose of caffeine, does it really matter which coffee I choose to buy? Of course it does. Starbucks and many other businesses that benefit from the sale of niche, high-quality products would not be in business if quality was not important. Luxury car brands wouldn't be so prevalent on the road, either. Particularly in some areas of our life, quality is important. After all, you wouldn't want to trust a first-year medical student with your upcoming gall bladder surgery or a paralegal in your subsequent medical malpractice suit. The higher the stakes, the more quality matters.

If quality matters so much, then why do we pay so little attention to it in the aspects of our life in which it is the most critical? The average adult needs at least seven hours of sleep a night. But according to recent Gallup polls, four out of every ten Americans get six hours or less than this each night on average.[2] Is the time we sacrifice from our sleep of higher quality? In some cases, yes, but in many other cases the answer is no (unless you value online shopping and scanning Facebook more than your sleep!). Sometimes, we simply take the path of least resistance rather than invest effort into deciding what is really in our best interest. Let's face it, choosing quality over quantity is not always the easy choice.

Why is the choice not easy? For one, quantity is more tangible than quality in many instances. Let's take your salary or wage, for example. It's pretty easy to appreciate that making $50,000 a year is better than making $40,000 a year. That's a no-brainer, right? But what if the higher-salaried job required you to work on the weekends several times a year? What if the lower-salaried position offered unlimited snacks and refreshments during work hours? What if you were surrounded by colleagues you loathed and in the other by people who inspired you? These factors are less tangible in nature when making value-based decisions, but clearly, they greatly affect quality.

---

2 Jeffrey M. Jones, "In U.S., 40 percent get less than recommended amount of sleep," GallupPoll.com, 2013, http://www.gallup.com/poll/166553/less-recommended-amount-sleep.aspx.

If the intangibles offer significant value to a situation, then they can make up for other shortcomings, like in this instance a lower salary.

The second reason we might choose quantity over quality is our propensity to ignore the long-term consequences of our actions. Take Americans' savings habits, for instance. Based on recent surveys, seven out of every ten Americans have less than $1,000 saved at any given time. Even if earnings increase, these figures don't significantly change. It would thus appear that many people choose more quantity now rather than higher quality later. The same applies to relationships. Do you know of a friend or family member who stays in a bad relationship simply because they have known the person for many years? This might be seen as committed and admirable, but the poor quality of the relationship can detract from life's value for everyone over time.

The third (and perhaps most common) reason we choose quantity over quality is cultural. I don't mean to say that our culture does not value quality, but a significant emphasis is placed on having more. We live in a consumption society, and buying and having more is often equated with feelings of success. In fact, many people make purchases to overcome feelings of low self-esteem or a sense of inadequacy. In other instances, "more" is used as a yardstick by which to measure our success against others. If I have a jet ski and a boat, and my neighbor only has a jet ski, then the perception is that I am more successful . . . even if my credit cards are maxed, my boat is in the shop more often than it's on the water, and I spend more time at work away from my family.

Examples of our consumptive tendencies are everywhere. A childhood friend of mine always dreamed of one day living in a large house. One day, after finally landing a well-paying job, he scraped together his savings and leveraged his position to get the highest mortgage he could in order to have his so-called dream home. He thought the day he became the owner of his new five-thousand-square-foot home would be the best day of his life. And in some ways, it was. But within a few months, the house became more of an albatross than a godsend. The lawn had to be mowed every week; pest control services ordered; and minor repairs and changes seemed to be never ending. In addition, he was having to sign up for any overtime available to help with these additional costs. He had the "more" of what he wanted, but his quality of life took a turn for the worse. My friend now rents a large urban apartment and is much happier.

In many instances where we must make a choice, both options usually offer some benefits. This is the case with the quantity versus quality debate. Certainly, in some cases, more IS better. But not always. Quality matters. The problem is not in our ability to appreciate this fact but instead in our ability to recognize, appreciate, and value its role in enhancing our lives. This is particularly true in the more critical aspects of our lives such as our careers, our relationships, and our activities. By paying attention to what provides us with a real sense of value, we can make better decisions that will guide us to the quality of life we truly desire.

The Process of Quality Control

What comes to mind when you think of quality control? If you're like most people, quality control is a buzz word for continuous improvement in organizations and businesses. It is associated with efficiency, reduced waste, optimal use of resources, and a product or service that meets specifications. Given the situations where you might have applied quality control measures, the process of quality control might sound pretty unexciting. But consider these same descriptions as they might relate to your own life. What if you could improve the quality of your job decisions, relationships, and the use of your time by applying the same type of process?

Before we go further into applying quality control to your personal life, we first need to understand exactly what quality control is. Certainly, the name alone is descriptive . . . we are controlling a situation and outcome for higher quality results. But how is this accomplished? What determines what is a desirable quality and what is not? Do we focus only on the outcome or on the steps along the way? What do we do if quality is found to be lacking? And how do we make sure the changes we make improve quality down the road? The quality control process tries to answer all of these questions.

Companies use several models for controlling quality in production and operations. Ever since the 1970s when Japanese companies used quality control methods to take the lead in the global automotive industry, an abundance of research and theories have been published about how best to control quality within businesses. As a result, significant advances have been made within the corporate setting to improve the quality of operations and productions. And depending on the type of product or service produced and the type of business you have, different approaches might work better than others.

Understanding that some nuances exist from business to business, five basic steps are essential to the quality control process. These five steps involve defining, measuring, analyzing, strategizing, and reassessing, or DMASR. Any business examining the quality of a process or product goes through each of these steps, at least to some degree, to provide consistency, reliability, efficiency, and high quality. In doing so, the business is better able to predict costs and offer the best product or service to its customers.

Let's break down these essential steps of quality control a bit further. The first step involves defining a quality standard for whatever outcome or behavior you are considering. Perhaps you define a quality standard as having only one product with a defect for every thousand made. Or maybe your standard of high quality is reducing the time of production to less than five minutes per product. Regardless of the standards you choose, they must be defined in tangible terms. Why? So you can perform the second step of the quality control process . . . measuring. If a quality standard is not well defined, then measuring the success of actual performance of it becomes quite difficult.

Once quality standards have been defined, and after these standards are used to measure actual performance, the next step involves analyzing results. Did performance meet the quality standard? If not, why not? What contributed to its failure in meeting the standard? How could performance be changed to improve the outcome? The analysis step of the quality control process requires you to take a step back and reflect on potential shortcomings and pitfalls in the process. This step is critical because it then offers you the ability to move on to the next step, which involves the development of strategies and potential solutions for any quality mishaps. Just as defining and measuring are closely associated in the DMASR process, analysis and strategy formation are as well.

This brings us to the final step of the quality control process . . . reassessment. Without reassessment, continual improvement in quality cannot be achieved. How can you know if your analysis and strategies were effective without a reassessment? You can't. The "R" of DMASR thus brings us back to where we started. Once you have reassessed, you may need to reconsider how you define your quality standards, or you may determine that a different way to measure quality is needed. You might also come to a different conclusion from your analysis and choose different strategies if your reassessment failed to improve quality to your liking. Thus, the quality control process is a never-ending cycle helping us to perpetually enhance quality.

The DMASR process begins with defining your quality standards, but even before that, quality must be defined as well. In fact, quality must be defined in precise terms, otherwise it becomes impossible to know when it is achieved. This might sound pretty straightforward, but in practice, it can be quite challenging. What might represent quality for one company may not be the same for another.

Let's take our coffee example again. The quality standards for Starbucks coffee beans are significantly different than those for the Maxwell House division of the Kraft-Heinz Corporation. The same considerations apply to your life as well. What you value in a career and a relationship will likely be quite different than someone else's.

According to Merriam-Webster, quality is defined as the degree of excellence present.[3] There is only one problem . . . what might be seen as excellence by me may not be seen as excellence by you. Certainly, levels of quality for some things can be agreed upon. For example, a food product contaminated with bacteria would be

---

3 Merriam-Webster dictionary, "Definition of quality," 2017, https://www.merriam-webster.com/dictionary/quality.

uniformly perceived as poor quality, and a luxury sports car that is fuel efficient, high speed, and enduring would likely be universally seen as high quality. But this is not true for everything. Not everyone thinks Starbucks coffee is high quality, and not everyone thinks Maxwell House brand is poor quality. With this in mind, quality must be defined according to your own personal values and opinions. Only you know what represents high and low quality when it comes to your life.

Defining quality also extends beyond a specific outcome. In addition to assessing quality of the end result, quality must also be defined in relation to the steps required to reach this destination. Starbucks might value the coffee brewed from Peruvian coffee beans, but if the steps required to get these beans from Peru take twice as long, cost twice as much, and result in twice as much waste, then the end result might not be worth it. By the same token, you might want a job that pays twice as much, but the time you must spend in education, training, and experience may not be worth pursuing the career. Even if they are, then the number of hours per week required by the job may result in opportunity costs to do other things important to you in your life. In any quality control process, quality must be well defined in order to know if quality is being achieved or not.

Sometimes, defining quality can be one of the most challenging aspects of the quality control process. But at the same time, identifying which factors influence quality for better or worse can also be difficult. For example, in the oil and gas industry, we might choose to put another inspector along a production line to make sure standards are being met. But in doing so, the extra time required for this additional inspection step delays production times and negatively affects delivery services. The added inspection is supposed to enhance quality, but instead, it makes overall quality worse.

Let's say you had to complete a business report by a certain date. Because you received the data relatively late, you hurried through the report, making lots of typos and grammatical mistakes. However, all the important information was included in the report. You then had a choice. You could submit the report on time (with the grammatical errors), or you could polish up the report and turn it in late. Assuming that receipt of the report was linked to a quality outcome for your company, you would have to determine whether timeliness of the report was more important than grammatical accuracy. In some cases, time is of the essence, but in others, professionalism might be more critical. Which factor is best linked to a true quality outcome?

For these reasons, a great deal of time in the quality control process is spent in defining quality and its related factors. Like a ship's compass, good quality control metrics provide the means to identify when things are off course. The quality control process is therefore only as good as its ability to measure whether quality standards are being met.

The final steps in the quality control process involve developing new strategies to make a change and examining whether these changes work. For example, if a company's analysis has shown that defects are occurring too often, then a different approach is needed to improve the situation. And while logic and analysis may suggest a specific change is needed, the proof will only be in the pudding. Businesses must reevaluate the entire process again after changes are made to be sure the problems have been corrected. In many cases, what should have worked may not; and in rare instances, solutions make things worse. Feedback is essential to ensure continuous progress toward quality.

For the most part, quality control is fairly straightforward, but like many things, the deeper you look, the more complex things can become. Some companies have a set of goals that do not necessarily align well with the company's vision or values. Even if goals are attained, quality will probably not be realized . . . at least for that particular company. Similarly, identifying what factors are linked to good quality and which are associated with bad quality can be difficult. Many of these factors may be hard to appreciate. Then, there is the problem of trying to measure quality. Consider the acronym

"GIGO," or garbage-in, garbage-out. If you have poor measurement systems, then you won't truly know when quality is achieved or not. These can be real obstacles in pursuing quality control, but they are not the only ones. Sometimes, quality goals, related factors, and measurements are accurate, but companies may have a hard time figuring out how to improve various tasks and activities in order to achieve better quality. In other instances, a company may assume it has dealt with the problem, but it never goes back to reassess whether the solution actually worked. And sometimes, there is simply a resistance to change, even though the change would be positive.

Regardless which quality control method your company might use or whether you are familiar with it, the process is, for the most part, intuitive and simple. To reiterate, you simply define, measure, analyze, strategize, and reassess (DMASR). But this process is not simply for companies, as you will soon see.

Making Quality Control Personal

In the oil and gas industry, I have come to appreciate the pervasive attention to quality not only in industries and businesses but also in every aspect of life. Certainly, customer service quality, product quality, and quality of production are common buzzwords in business, but other sectors are embracing these concepts as well. For example, in healthcare, Medicare payment systems are being redesigned to reward doctors and hospitals for quality outcomes rather on the number of services they provide. Quality control is not simply for big businesses and corporations anymore.

Let's assume you are going out to eat in a city where you have never been. How would you choose which restaurant to eat at? Today, this is simple. You would likely search any number of websites or social media platforms to examine what others have said about the quality of food, the service, the price, etc. In essence, when you assess this way you have performed a quality control experiment. You defined the quality desired (price, cuisine, customer experiences); you examined metrics regarding those definitions (site rankings, customer responses, need for reservations); analyzed your findings (results of metrics, geographic proximity, level of hunger; personal budget); and developed a strategy (choice of restaurant, time, locations). And possibly, you will then render your own opinion online of your own experience at that restaurant.

Now, let's expand this concept even further. What if you decided to apply this same quality control process to important life decisions? To some extent, you probably already do in informal (and possibly incomplete) ways. Perhaps you are considering going back to school at night and taking online classes. Maybe you are thinking about starting your own company. Or you might be struggling to end a long-term relationship with someone. In each of these instances, you have defined some level of quality that you desire, have determined this desire is currently not being met, and developed a strategy to make your desire a reality. In short, this is a quality control process of sorts.

Over the course of my career, I have tackled many entrepreneurial pursuits as side businesses. Why? Because something was lacking for me at the time. Eventually I came to the conclusion that the mental process I undertook each time resembled the quality control methods I now use at the oil and gas company. Initially, I would compare my process more to a cost and benefit analysis. I would make a list of the pros and the cons, and then determine if the adventure was worth pursuing.

The problem with my cost-benefit analyses was that they were too limited and superficial. I would cite as many advantages and disadvantages as I could, and I would even assign a weighted strength to each one before tallying the results. But the analysis still lacked the level of depth I needed to help me feel confident about my final decision.

Over time, I developed a consistent yet dynamic way to apply the quality control process to specific areas of my life. And guess what . . . it works! From job decisions to life decisions, this process has made a tremendous impact on the quality of my life.

I call this approach the Quality Core Process, or QCP for short. The QCP does require some investments and participation on your part in order to get the most of life. What are the primary investments? Mainly your time and effort. Imagine if you were asked to define what represented quality in someone else's life. Even if it were your sibling or best friend, you could no more effectively help make quality choices for someone else than I could for you. Thus, the benefits of the QCP require your involvement. However, your participation is an important investment in yourself.

Second, there is no right or wrong way to implement the Quality Core Process. The answers you provide for each step of the QCP depend on your preferences, priorities, and values. If you make a mistake and the quality of your life doesn't improve, simply reevaluate. Reevaluation is an inherent and essential step within the Quality Core Process. Perfection is not guaranteed, but continual improvement and increasing levels of quality are, as long as you continue a cycle of reassessment and reanalysis. With each additional application, the QCP refines the level of quality for each area in your life that you explore.

The QCP has the ability to make a tremendous impact on your life even while making incremental improvements in quality. Think about someone who is overweight and is able to lose twenty pounds. Though they may still need to lose several more pounds to reach their ideal weight, the initial loss makes them feel much healthier. In the same way, a 5 to 10 percent improvement in quality can make a great deal of difference in your life. The QCP does not try to completely reinvent your life. Instead, it seeks to help you reorganize your life so your pursuit of quality (and its presence in your life) is increased.

Last, be aware that improvements in quality of life occur not only in the final outcomes but in the processes along the way. This was an important revelation I had while employing quality control in the workplace. If you want quality outcomes, you have to improve the quality in each step of production. And when each step is improved, the cumulative effects on quality are not simply the sum of each part but much greater. The same holds true when applying the QCP to your life. It's as much about the journey (if not more) as it is about the final results. In other words, the QCP offers a comprehensive approach to improving your life's quality.

The QCP can be applied to your life as a general overview or in more detail to each specific area of interest. For example, you may decide to use the process to help create a general guide to a more qualitative life, or you may elect to dig a little deeper into specific life categories. Whether you are trying to determine whether to advance your career in your current organization or completely shift gears toward another career pursuit, the QCP can help. Likewise, it can be used to foster quality decisions about better health, better relationship, better spending habits, and where your time, thought, and energy are invested. To whatever extent you wish to use it, the QCP offers you the means to enhance the level of quality in your life, both now and throughout your lifetime.

Chapter 2

The Quality Core Process

I have spent nearly all my life in Wyoming, and as you might imagine, hunting is a fairly common sport in the state. One of my friends, who is an avid sportsman, often uses the phrase, "You don't need a barrel of buckshot to kill a squirrel." In his own unique way, he is simply saying a more targeted approach is better for some things. Rather than trying to tackle everything all at once, focusing on a specific area can sometimes be more productive. By choosing the right approach for the right goal, you are more likely to use your time and effort more wisely.

While focusing on a specific area is helpful in some situations, in many instances a more generalized approach is helpful. I am sure everyone has heard someone described as not being able to see the forest for the trees. The person is so focused on the specific details that they lose sight of the big picture. In my experience as a quality control expert, I have seen errors made in both circumstances. I have witnessed a project fall short of expectations because too much time was spent on a single part of the production process. And I have seen important steps in production overlooked because too much emphasis was placed on the final metrics only. Both the forest and tree approach are important . . . but the key is to know when to take each one.

In applying the Quality Core Process, you should always pursue both a general and specific approach in assessing your life. Assessing the quality of your overall life is important, as it helps put various pieces of your life into perspective. Likewise, a general approach helps you develop goals and objectives related to your values and beliefs that will permeate all areas of your life. At the same time, applying the QCP in a more targeted way to specific aspects of your life can help you make progress in areas that you see as priorities. Both applications are important and add value to your life.

In this chapter, we will consider a general approach in applying the Quality Core Process. As you will see in later chapters, the generalized approach offers a broader view of what you define as quality in your life while providing some overall guidelines that you can adopt in all areas of your life. At the same time, the general approach will likely identify some of the more focused areas of your life that deserve attention. Subsequent chapters can help you apply the QCP to some of the more common targeted areas, but for now, let's set our sights on the forest instead of the trees.

Step 1 – Define Your Standards

In recalling the standard QCP, the first step in the DMASR structure is to define what quality is. But how do you define quality personally? You can define quality any way you like, but through trial and error, I have found that taking a business approach toward defining quality can be incredibly helpful. After all, successful companies have been competing with one another for years on the basis of cost and quality, so it only stands to reason that their ability to define and assess quality has some merit.

So how do successful companies define quality and quality standards? From a general perspective, quality is typically defined in what I like to call a company's manifesto . . . their mission statement, their vision, and their values. Businesses that dedicate time and energy into refining these quality perspectives and aligning them well with a company's core competencies are much more likely to experience success in the long run. And guess what . . . the same is true for you in relation to your own life. By establishing your own overriding mission statement, vision, and value system, your chances to achieve a high-quality life increase significantly.

So, let's begin with your personal mission statement. How do you come up with a personal mission statement? Concentrate on a single, overriding theme in life that you associate with high quality. Perhaps you relate quality to having many strong family relationships in your life, or maybe quality is linked to a legacy or acts of charity. Your view of a high-quality life might simply be one that has little conflict. How you define quality is not important, but identifying your life's specific theme linked to quality is.

Experts who help companies develop mission statements suggest that these should be simple and concise statements. In fact, mission statements should be eight words or less, according to some. One approach encourages businesses to use a mission statement formula consisting of a verb, a target, and an outcome.[4] For example, my personal mission statement using this formula is, "To achieve ever-increasing knowledge to empower others." With this mission statement, the verb is "to achieve," the target is "ever-increasing knowledge," and the outcome is "to empower others." And I only used seven words total. What mission statement works for you as an overall guide to a high-quality life?

Ideally, mission statements should be relatively constant throughout your life to provide consistent direction, but even companies will sometimes reassess their long-term mission. Regardless, dedicating adequate time in determining your own personal mission statement can help provide you with a more lasting quality compass and direction. When choosing a verb, consider one that reflects clear action. When identifying a target of the action, try to narrow down the target to

---

4 Kevin Starr, "The eight-word mission statement," *The Stanford Social Innovation Review*, 2012, https://ssir.org/articles/entry/the_eight_word_mission_statement.

make it real and tangible. And when choosing an outcome, certainly make sure it represents something that defines quality for your life. Good mission statements have all of these qualities.

In essence, a mission statement describes your purpose in life. What is your reason for living? What truly gives your life meaning? What are you pursuing in order to make your life a high-quality life? Think of a mission statement as your way of defining quality standards for your life so that your life has a deeper sense of fulfillment. By creating a successful mission statement, you will have a clearer perspective on where you want your life to go.

Once you have established a quality mission statement, the next step is to develop a vision statement for your high-quality life. If mission statements define your life's purpose, then vision statements paint a picture of what that life will look like when you attain it. Your vision is therefore a more future-oriented statement that depicts where you want to be in five years, ten years, or even at the end of your life.

How do you create a vision statement, and how does this highlight your defined quality standards? Think of a vision statement as what your life would look like if you achieved all your goals in the future. According to my mission statement, "To achieve ever-increasing knowledge to empower others," you can appreciate my overall goals. My vision statement is therefore, "To empower every person to pursue a high-quality life through deeper personal understanding."

The perspective of this statement is futuristic in nature (and to some extent timeless), and it offers a long-standing vision to pursue. At the same time, you can appreciate that the mission statement aligns well with the ultimate vision. When determining your vision statement, be sure that your mission and vision support one another and that both pursue the quality of life you truly want.

At this point, we have now defined our life's purpose and our life's vision as it pertains to the high-quality life we desire. The final step in defining our quality standards involves identifying key personal values that we must follow in pursuing a high-quality life. Suppose Bernie Madoff's mission statement was to raise people's confidence about their future retirement. For years, Madoff achieved this purpose. Or maybe Lance Armstrong's mission was to outperform all other cyclists in the Tour de France. Lance definitely accomplished his mission. But in both of these cases, their missions were achieved through unethical and illegal behaviors.

When we talk about living a high-quality life, our personal values matter. The journey is as important as the final outcome, and therefore, we need to identify our core values when determining quality standards. We need to know our life's purpose and long-term vision as it relates to quality, but we also need to acknowledge the way we plan to achieve these quality standards. A true quality life is only realized when our goals and objectives are achieved through authentic behaviors that are also quality focused.

What are your core values? Honesty, integrity, respect for others? Transparency, accountability, loyalty? Just as quality standards and definitions can vary from person to person, priority values can vary as well. But one thing is certain. It is impossible to pursue a high-quality life while adopting behaviors that conflict with your underlying beliefs and values. Quality demands congruence, and in order to realize a high-quality life, you must properly align your values, behaviors, mission, and vision with your definition of quality in mind. Taking the time to define your values well provides you with a strong foundation upon which to pursue the high-quality life you deserve.

Step 2 – Measure Up

When I was twenty-five years of age and the quality control manager in the family business became ill, forcing him to take an extended leave of absence, I had been working for our company for years, but to say I was ready to assume this position was quite a stretch. Despite my lack of knowledge and experience, I embraced my new responsibilities and immersed myself in dozens of texts that explained the quality control process. Before long, I was designing pressure equipment and monitoring quality control according to industry standards for the company. I even became a Certified Welding Inspector, which is considered a significant accomplishment within the field of quality control.

During this transitional period in my life, I realized the importance of being able to hold something against a quality standard. From the perspective of my family's business, I needed that standard in order to determine whether or not the company was performing well or if changes were needed. From an inspector's position, I needed these same standards upon which to base my opinions and conclusions. Standards are essential when addressing quality. Not only do they define the level of quality required, but they also provide the means by which quality can be measured.

In Step 1 of the QCP, we defined personal standards of quality for your life based on your mission statement, vision statement, and list of personal values. In defining these standards, you determined a clear direction in pursuing a high-quality life. However, at the same time, these statements and standards are somewhat abstract with little to offer in terms of discrete metrics. While these definitions of personal quality are essential, they lack the level of detail needed to precisely identify whether a standard is met or not. In other words, your mission statement, vision, and values offer a general compass to guide you, but you still need a way to measure whether your efforts meet these standards.

Step 2 of the QCP therefore involves identifying ways to measure your pursuits against the standards you have defined. How do you do this? By compiling a list of specific goals and objectives that exemplify the same quality standards you identified in Step 1. Goals are useful because they offer all-or-none measurements by which you can assess your personal success. If you do not meet your goals, then you can easily reassess and revise. And if you attain your goals, then they provide a place from which to develop future goals.

When creating goals related to your personal quality standards, some rules do apply. First, goals have to be measurable. What does this mean? Consider the goal, "I will become a better student." While this is a wonderful goal, it is hardly measurable. What metric determines whether you are a better student or not? A better goal statement might be, "I will maintain a grade average above a B+," or "I will study every day for at least two hours." These goals are clearly measurable and allow you to determine whether your personal quality standards are being met.

Second, goals need to have a time limit. In our example above, how long are you supposed to maintain a grade average above a B+ or study daily for at least two hours? A week, a month, the entire school year, or indefinitely? Placing a time limit on a goal is essential when pursuing a high-quality life. Without time parameters, goals can quickly lose their priority due to a reduced sense of urgency.

In contrast, goals that must be accomplished within a specific time period can greatly enhance motivations by adding an accountability measure. If you don't think this works, try telling a dozen people about a goal and its associated time limit. You will be amazed at the level of motivation you will have in attaining that goal once everyone else knows about it.

The last caveat related to goal setting is rather intuitive but at the same time challenging. As you might expect, goals need to align with your defined quality standards. But sometimes, listing goals that effectively accomplish your quality standard can be difficult. For example, the mission statement listed previously sought to achieve deeper knowledge to empower others, but what goals achieve this deeper knowledge AND can be used to empower others? A formal education might be one way, but in what field of study? Attending empowerment seminars might be another reasonable goal, but will you be able to empower others simply because you are empowered?

To highlight this point further, let me share a story about a friend of mine. My friend has always been a runner, and he routinely placed rather high in the 5K and 10K races he entered. But for whatever reason, he started smoking cigarettes at the age of thirty-five. What began as an occasional cigarette in the evening gradually grew into a couple of packs a week. But all the while, he continued to run as he always had.

A few years later, he decided to quit smoking. After trying several different traditional strategies, he repeatedly failed to accomplish this goal. Finally, he decided to take a completely different approach. Having never even attempted a half marathon, he signed up to run a marathon. Two months into his training he had quit smoking entirely. The increased physical demands on his body had completely taken away any desire he had to smoke.

The point of this story is that you sometimes have to be creative in defining your personal goals in order to best align them with your quality standards. My friend had previously set goals that were measurable and had a time limit, but he repeatedly fell short of the goal. But once he adopted a different (and unique) approach, he was able to quit smoking by pursuing the goal to run a marathon. For this reason, identifying various factors that might be associated with your quality values, vision, and mission can be a good exercise. For him, increased exercise capacity and avoidance of tobacco were linked, both of which were part of his definition of a high-quality life. He simply considered both of these factors together in establishing a new strategy to attain his goal to quit smoking.

Step 3 – Analyze Where You Are

You now have your own definition of quality standards, as well as specific goals that measure these pursuits in your life. Step 3 of the

QCP involves applying this information to your life so you have a good idea of where things are in the present. The only way to know if you are making progress toward your quality goals is by assessing where you are at the beginning. At the same time, analyzing your current situation also allows you to identify those things that make you unique so you can leverage these characteristics to your advantage and success.

In the QCP, the analysis step involves three specific exercises to help you assess your present situation and unique character. These include a self-inventory of your strengths and weaknesses, an assessment of your current life stage and generational influences, and an evaluation that past life experiences have had on your point of view. By performing each of these exercises, you will gain a much deeper understanding of what quality means to you and the areas where you can make improvements in your life.

Let's start with your self-inventory. Have you ever heard of a SWOT analysis? Companies frequently perform these analyses to help them develop strategies to accomplish their goals. SWOT stands for strengths, weaknesses, opportunities, and threats. All of these are important, for both a company and for you as an individual. But two of these categories are related to you personally, while the other two reflect the environment in which you exist. Specifically, your strengths and weaknesses are things unique to you, but opportunities and threats highlight things affecting your immediate environment. Likewise, strengths and weaknesses are often more easily changed, whereas opportunities and threats are often out of your control.

While strengths and weaknesses are part of your self-inventory, opportunities and threats are better to consider in relation to your goals. For example, if you have a goal to finish college within the next two years, opportunities might include online coursework, student loans, employer-based incentives, and others. At the same time, threats might include financial obstacles, limited time, and other work or family responsibilities. With each of the goals, you can assess the opportunities and threats that facilitate or hinder their successful completion, respectively. This will help you examine where your strengths might be best utilized and where you can best minimize your weaknesses.

In terms of your strengths and weaknesses, ask yourself three important questions: 1) What activities give you the most joy, and which ones give you the least? 2) What are the activities in which you clearly excel, and which ones are a constant struggle? 3) Last, what activities seem to cause time to fly, and which ones seem to make time drag? Strengths tend to be associated with positive emotions (confidence, pride, joy, self-esteem). Positive results often occur when performing activities that utilize your strengths. And time flies when your positive assets are being used to perform a task or activity. In contrast, the opposite tends to be true for weaknesses. These often evoke negative feelings, can be commonly associated with poor outcomes, and time can drag when tasks exposing your weaknesses occur. These three simple questions are quite effective in identifying your core strengths and weaknesses.

The second part of this self-analysis step involves evaluating your current life stage and generational influences. What does this mean? Consider this for a moment . . . when you were in high school or college (perhaps you still are), how would you characterize a high-quality life? What about when you reached middle age with a family and children? What about late in life after you have retired? As individuals, our human development is ongoing, and each life stage shifts our perspective to some degree, identifying different priorities along the way. Therefore, part of a comprehensive self-inventory requires examining your current and future life stages so that you pursue those things you see as being important and of high quality.

As part of this life stage assessment, it is also helpful to appreciate the effect past life experiences and generational influences have had on you. For example, baby boomers are typically more ambitious, prefer a single career, and have a strong work ethic. In contrast, millennials tend to expect change and diversity, commonly explore multiple careers, and desire work that is more personally meaningful than financially rewarding. Based on the generation in which you grew up, you likely adopted specific preferences, dislikes, as well as values that affect how you perceive quality. While these revelations do not mean that your perception of quality is better or worse than someone else's, they do provide you with key insights about why you value the things you do.

Similarly, past experiences can also affect how you perceive quality. For example, someone who has tragically lost both their parents early in life may place greater emphasis on family and family relationships in defining quality of life when compared to another person. Or someone who is the first to attend college out of their family may think higher education best represents quality of life. Neither of these views are right or wrong, but they help you understand why you value what you value, and why you perceive quality the way you do. This is important when analyzing your current life in relation to your ultimate goals.

Once you have taken an inventory of your strengths and weaknesses, examined your life stage and generational influences, and appreciated how your past affects your present views of quality, you are now better equipped to analyze your current state of affairs in relation to your quality definitions and goals. Consider the following questions as you put this information together:

- What do you value in your life now? Will this change as you get older?

- How is your view of quality affected by your life's past experiences? Is this view something you accept or need to change?
- What personality traits, skills, and abilities do you have that can be used to meet your goals for a high-quality life?
- What personality traits and inabilities reflect weaknesses that require attention to meet your goals?
- How can you use your strengths to take advantage of life opportunities?
- How can you minimize your weaknesses to avoid potential threats for a high-quality life?

After reflecting on these questions and others, go back and look at your mission statement, vision statement, and values. Do your answers to these questions align with your definitions of quality in your life? Also, take another look at your goals for realizing a high-quality life. Are your goals realistic, measurable, and timely? What specific things will you need to change or take advantage of in order to achieve these goals? Take your time in answering these questions because they allow you the opportunity to see discrepancies between your definition and standards of quality with the realities of your life. And this, in turn, will help guide you in Step 4 of the Quality Core Process.

Step 4 – Develop a Quality-of-Life Strategy

Over the course of my career, I have pursued several entrepreneurial enterprises. While several steps are required when considering such a pursuit, one of the initial tasks involves developing a solid business plan. If you have ever created such a plan, you know the level of detail a business plan requires if you are going to truly pursue success. From the company's structure, to a market analysis, to a structured timeline, a business plan provides a guide by which specific steps can be taken to realize your dream. If these steps are constructed well and are based on rational strategies, then you can use the plan as a road map for years to come.

Interestingly, creating strategies to realize a high-quality life is a lot like developing a business plan. Having now implemented the QCP to better appreciate how you define quality in your life, and by analyzing your current life situation, the strategy phase requires a step-by-step process by which you pursue the changes necessary to attain your quality goals. As the quality control manager in the oil and gas business, developing strategies for positive change was an ongoing activity. But in each instance, specific steps were identified that helped us move from the present to the future with higher quality in mind.

Having said this, this part of the QCP requires detailed consider-ations when determining which steps to take and when. My friend who pursued marathon training to quit smoking initially outlined several step-by-step strategies to quit smoking before deciding to run the farther distance. Though all of the strategies were logical, they failed to be effective for one reason or another. In time, however, he kept tweaking his strategies until he arrived at one that was effective in accomplishing his goal.

Developing an effective strategy to improve quality in your life should therefore be seen as a work in progress. The first attempt may not knock a home run out of the park, but if it gets you on base, then you are making progress. From this point of view, you should carefully examine each task and variable that might affect your ability to reach your goals. Then, a specific strategy to change the variables or tasks should be developed in an organized, systematic way. Each step of a strategy should build upon another until ultimately you reach your quality goal. And if the completion of a step fails to provide the result you expected, you may need a new strategy.

Suppose you wanted to donate more of your time to volunteering in a community organization that helped underprivileged children. What strategy would you adopt to realize this goal? The steps involved in your strategy might include contacting the community organization and seeing what opportunities were available, and then reviewing your schedule and commitments to see when you could volunteer. Having already completed an analysis step of the QCP, you identified that one of your weaknesses was inconsistency in effort. With this in mind, you add another step in your strategy to find a partner with whom to volunteer so you are more likely to be held accountable. Perhaps you also recognized that one of your strengths was your social skills. So, your next step involved attending several social functions of the organization to establish better relationships. The more effort you exerted in developing a detailed step-by-step strategic plan, the more likely you were to attain your quality goal.

While the analysis and strategy steps of the QCP are designed to occur in tandem, sometimes these two steps require a bit of interplay in order to develop the best strategies possible. As we will soon discuss, the same level of interplay is often required between strategy formation and reassessment. Regardless, it remains important for you to invest time and energy in creating a stepwise strategy that pursues your quality goals based on the preceding steps of the Quality Core Process. This is how you best guide quality control in your life through continuous progress and improvement.

Step 5 – Reassess and Repeat

Have you ever read the poem entitled "There's a hole in my sidewalk" by Portia Nelson? It goes as follows:

> I walk down the street.
> There is a deep hole in the sidewalk.

I fall in.

I am lost . . . I am helpless.

It isn't my fault.

It takes forever to find a way out.

I walk down the same street.

There is a deep hole in the sidewalk.

I pretend I don't see it.

I fall in again.

I can't believe I am in the same place.

But, it isn't my fault.

It still takes me a long time to get out.

I walk down the same street.

There is a deep hole in the sidewalk.

I see it is there.

I still fall in. It's a habit.

My eyes are open.

I know where I am.

It is my fault. I get out immediately.

I walk down the same street.

There is a deep hole in the sidewalk.

I walk around it.

I walk down another street[5]

---

5 Portia Nelson, *There's a Hole in My Sidewalk: The Romance of Self-discovery* (New York, NY: Simon and Schuster, 2012).

The poem highlights beautifully the importance of reevaluation. As the author walks down her street and sidewalk, she continues to make the same mistake until finally she chooses to change her behavior. Only after reassessing the situation can she appreciate that she has control over the outcome and can alter her actions as a means to change it. But without reassessing the situation, the same result will continue to happen . . . over and over again.

In this poem, the hole and the sidewalk remain the same, but the author's actions change in order to achieve a different goal. But what if the situation was changing as well? In other words, what if a road crew came and filled up the hole, but heavy rains washed out another spot in the road several yards away? Or what if the author kept taking a different sidewalk even though the hole in the other sidewalk had been repaired? Indeed, her behavior changed as a result of proper reevaluation of self-actions in a stable environment, but behaviors also need to change when everything around us changes as well.

Not only is reassessment important in relation to the failure to achieve a quality goal, but it is also required continuously since everything around us is in a constant state of flux. Can you imagine trying to compete in business today using a telephone and fax without cellular service or the Internet? The quality of customer service would consistently be seen as poor when compared to your competitors. Without regularly performing reassessments of your quality definitions, goals, and strategies, you run the risk of becoming complacent in your pursuit of a high-quality life. While the other steps of the QCP are important in pursuing those aspects of your life that you consider priorities, the reassessment step is essential if you are to make continued progress.

At this point, you have spent a great deal of time defining what quality means to you, setting goals that help you realize quality in your life, and developing steps to meet those goals. You have even considered how your perspective of quality may change over time as your roles and responsibilities change. But it is also important to consider the effect that a changing world has on your perception of quality. The definition of quality does vary from person to person based on personal preferences and experiences, but your environment also exerts some effect on these perceptions.

Let's take a real-world example. Three decades ago, you would have likely gone into any restaurant or pub and found a small selection of domestic beers. A few places may have had a couple of token imported beers, but small batch, craft beers would have been a rarity. Now, think about restaurants and pubs today. How many places do you go that have at least a handful of craft beer selections? This is a perfect example of how our surroundings have changed your perspective of quality (of beers). The same could be applied to premium roast coffee, cable television offerings, or many other products and services. Similarly, our surroundings also affect how we see quality in our own lives.

The bottom line is that change demands reassessment. This change may occur as a result of something you do, or it may occur due to changes beyond your control in your environment. If you altered your behavior to achieve a quality goal in your life, reassessment is required to see if this change resulted in goal achievement. If you reached the goal, reassessment is required to see if the goal provided you with a greater sense of quality in your life. If not, reassessment of your quality definitions may be needed, or you may need to reassess your quality goals themselves. Only through reassessment will you be able to progressively refine your efforts to realize the highest quality life possible.

Likewise, reassessment is needed when things around you change. Suppose you failed to meet a quality goal. Reassessment of your effort or strategy may be required due to changes that occurred in your life situation. If you did attain a quality goal but it failed to provide you with a feeling of higher quality, then reassessing your situation may be needed here as well. When performing the reassessment step of the QCP, both internal and external evaluations are needed. Certainly, examine your thoughts, feelings, and efforts regarding quality in your life, but at the same time, take a look at whether your circumstances have changed as well.

So how do you reassess when using the Quality Core Process? What do you reassess? And in what order? When you get to the reassessment step of the process, first start with those things that are easiest to evaluate, and then move on to those areas that may be more challenging. For example, let's say you had a quality goal to start your own coffee shop within the year. The easiest way to reassess your pursuit of quality in your life is to see if you met this objective. That is why effectively defining your quality goals is so important. This makes it much easier to determine whether or not you're on the right track.

Once you have reassessed whether or not you have reached your goals, the next part of the reassessment process can be a little more difficult. If you did not meet your goals, why not? Perhaps you did not invest enough time, energy, or effort. Or perhaps you did, but your strategy and approach were all wrong. If you succeeded in meeting your goals, further reassessment is required here also. Did achieving your goal result in a higher-quality life based on your mission, vision, and values? If not, perhaps you need to reconsider your goals or even reassess your definitions of quality.

In essence, the reassessment step of the QCP moves from the more obvious to the less obvious. First, reassess whether you met your goals, then sequentially reevaluate your strategies to achieve these goals, the congruence between these goals and your perception of quality, and last, your definitions of quality. As you reassess these areas sequentially, you move from the more likely to the less likely areas where change is needed moving forward. And the more you perform this reassessment over time, the chance you will need to alter your definitions of quality and your goals will be less as well. Not only does the reassessment step help keep you moving in the right direction toward a high-quality life, but it also continually refines your perception of real quality.

In this chapter, we have outlined how you can use the QCP to define, measure, analyze, strategize, and reassess quality in your life. The approach has been to apply the QCP in a general way in order to provide you with an overview of how you perceive quality and a pervasive strategy in pursuing a higher-quality life. This chapter served two key purposes. First, it highlighted how to perform each step of the QCP overall. Second, it demonstrated how it can be used as a general guide toward enhanced fulfillment. In other words, we have used the QCP to better identify quality from a "forest" perspective as it applies to your life.

For some of you, this generalized application of the QCP may be enough to send you on a path toward enhanced life quality and personal fulfillment. But for others, this will be only a beginning. Now that you have used the QCP to define quality based on your personal mission, vision, and values in a general sense, you can now refine the process even further so that it can be used in more specific areas of your life. Once you have mastered the ability to perform each step of the QCP in a few of these areas, it will become second nature. Before you know it, you will be applying it to every area of your life so you can truly reach your greatest potential.

In the next section, we will discuss how to apply the QCP in a more specific manner to key areas of your life. Subsequent chapters will highlight how the process is applied in the more common areas where quality is a priority, including health, career, finances, relationships, and even your daily thoughts. As you read each of the chapters, think about how the general QCP presented in this chapter is being adapted to the more focused topic being presented. As you gain an appreciation of this adaptation, you can then be creative in applying the process to any area of your life where you desire higher quality.

SECTION 2:

Applying QCP to Everyday Life

Chapter 3

Quality Core in Your Career

Do you like your job? If you are like many Americans, the answer is probably no. According to some surveys, over half of Americans are unhappy in their current jobs and positions at work.[6] However, the number of people seeking new jobs or careers is not nearly as high as expected. Though one reason for this discrepancy may be that all jobs cause some level of dissatisfaction, another reason is that we are simply too busy and distracted to consider other options. After all, over a third of our waking hours during our working years are spent on the job, and with today's mobile technologies, most of us continue to be engaged at some level with our work in our "off" hours as well. Isn't it a shame to spend so much of our time doing something that fails to add quality to our lives?

Unfortunately, lost opportunities for a more rewarding career represent only one side of the quality-of-life coin. You may not like your job and choose not to do anything about that, but many people

---

6 Susan Adams, "Most Americans unhappy at work," *Forbes*, 2014, https://www.forbes.com/sites/susanadams/2014/06/20/most-americans-are-unhappy-at-work/#3c48eec9341a.

also have jobs that cause them an abundance of stress. As many as 40 percent of workers in the US describe their work as stressful.[7] Perhaps a vacation would help reduce these levels of stress, but workers relinquish more than half of all vacation days each year.[8] Not only do many people persevere in jobs that are stressful and disappointing, but they also fail to take advantage of some of the perks these jobs provide! This is not a good strategy for pursuing a high-quality life.

In an effort to attain a more fulfilling and rewarding life, performing a quality control examination of your short-term and long-term career plans is important. This not only pertains to the company manager or coffee shop barista. It also applies to homemakers, charity volunteers, and many other lifetime pursuits. Not every career has a salary attached to it, but all careers can benefit from the Quality Core Process.

Step 1 – Define Your Dream Job

Let's assume you have worked for a company for several years. You don't really like the job, and the opportunities for career advancement are limited. Your best bet for moving upward in the company involves someone else's unexpected misfortune or an unlikely acquisition by a larger firm. Neither scenario offers much hope for the immediate

---

7 Harris Interactive, "Stress in the workplace," American Psychological Association, 2011, https://www.apa.org/news/press/releases/phwa-survey-summary.pdf.
8 Jessica Dickler, "U.S. workers forfeit half of their vacation days," CNBC.com, 2017, http://www.cnbc.com/2017/06/19/u-s-workers-forfeit-half-their-vacation-time.html.

future. So, you decide to explore your options elsewhere. Where do you look? Do you pursue the same career path, or do you leverage your skills into some other area? You might even take the bold move to start your own business. In order to answer these questions, however, you have to define what type of career can provide you with real satisfaction and fulfillment.

Asking such questions is often as far as many people get when they find themselves in such a position. For some, the risk of taking a chance on a new path is overwhelming. For others, life is simply too busy, and they are distracted from focusing on the change needed. And naturally, both the risks and distractions tend to accumulate the older we get. In some cases, the risks may not be worth changing career directions, but without evaluating your situation in detail, you cannot possibly know whether this is the case or not.

The first step in achieving a higher-quality life is in determining the career that you truly desire. Numerous career tests are available online and elsewhere to help individuals narrow down the list of jobs for which they are best suited. Examples of tests to help you better understand your personality include the Myers Briggs Type Indicator, DISC, and the Big Five Factor Model. Other tests, like the Kiersey Temperament Sorter, take this a step further and align personality types with categories of jobs. And the MAPP Career Assessment Test examines your temperament as well as your interests and skills to help determine your motivations for different jobs.[9] All of these are valuable tools, but often additional information is needed or the results may make things more complex than they need to be.

This is not to say exploring these career tools is not beneficial. Admittedly, I have taken several of these in exploring different career paths myself. I have learned a great deal about my personality by taking these tests, and I have come to appreciate some of my strengths, as well as my weaknesses. But through this process, I have also identified the three key areas that offer me the best guide in finding my ultimate dream job: my skills, my interests, and those pursuits that provide me with a deep sense of fulfillment. If you can target these three areas, then the chances you will accurately define your dream job is greatly enhanced.

So, what are your skills, interests, and fulfillments? These are fairly broad categories to consider, but at the same time, they offer a simple construct to define your dream job. After struggling with such matters, I developed six basic questions to help myself and others find answers.

Skills

- What do I do best (in my current job or past jobs)?
- What do my friends and colleagues say are my best talents?

---

9 G. Kim Dority, Rethinking Information Work: A Career Guide for Librarians and Other Information Professionals: A Career Guide for Librarians and Other Information Professionals, ABC-CLIO, 2016.

Interests

- Whose job among the people I know do I most envy?

- What activities cause me to completely lose track of time?

Fulfillment

- What activities make me feel good about myself?

- What tasks do I perform without any concern for compensation?

By pondering these questions, you will be more likely to come to some conclusions about the type of job and career you wish to pursue. Perhaps you are already on the right career path, or alternatively, you may need to make some drastic changes. Regardless, defining the core aspects of your dream job will establish a standard of quality in your career life. This standard will "set the bar" for all of your future decisions and actions about your employment options. In other words, the characteristics of your dream job will determine what represents real quality in your career pursuits. Once this has been defined, the rest of the QCP can then logically follow.

As with the general approach in using the QCP, feel free to also define a mission statement, vision, and set of guiding values in relation to your dream job or career. These can help you gauge which actions to take and which opportunities offer the best means for you to achieve your goals. Not every opportunity for advancement may be right for you in relationship to moving you from point A to B.

By having a career mission statement, a long-term vision, and an understanding of your own personal values, you will be better able to make wise decisions as it concerns your future career prospects.

Step 2 – Create Career Goals and Objectives

Once you have a good idea about the type of career you want to pursue, the next step in the QCP is to develop a set of measures that you can use to evaluate your progress. In business, quality control measures are those that accurately align with the standards that have been set. For instance, if an assembly line standard is to manufacture high-quality products, then the measure used might define a certain percentage of products made without defects. For instance, a company might say the quality standard has been met if a defective product occurs only once in every thousand products.

Unfortunately, this type of measurement doesn't usually work well in assessing your career progress, but creating specific career goals can. What goals can help you get the career you want? One might be to move into a management position within three years. Perhaps your goal might be to launch your own business before year's end. Or you might have a goal to enroll in school in order to acquire new skills needed for a job change. As you can see, none of these goals are endpoints in and of themselves, but they allow a measurement of progress toward your defined standards for your dream career.

In essence, they are stepping-stones along the path to your ultimate destination.

Setting goals is not necessarily hard, but it does take some effort to make sure your goals move you in the right direction. How can you be sure you create effective goals? I have found that most effective goals have a number of key characteristics. Using the mnemonic "MI-CAREER," you can create goals that will be more likely to get you to where you want to be.

- **M**easurable – any goal must be measurable in order to evaluate whether or not it has been attained.

- **I**maginative – Not all goals are obvious and straightforward. Sometimes creativity is needed to come up with the best goals to propel you forward.

- **C**hallenging – Your goals must motivate you and challenge you to push ahead.

- **A**chievable – Though challenging, goals must be achievable to avoid discouragement.

- **R**ealistic – Likewise, goals must be realistic to maintain motivation and enthusiasm.

- **E**xplicit – Goals need to be specific and precise. Vague goals can undermine your best efforts.

- **E**xciting – Make your goals exciting and inspiring. Let them help motivate you to your ultimate career vision.

- **R**ight timing – All goals must include a deadline. By having goals with the right timing, each goal can support another in helping you progress in your career pursuits.

Let's take an example of a career goal that would fit these criteria. Working in my family's business for many years, through my own efforts and through chance, I advanced quickly into higher-level management positions, but unfortunately, these were not the career choices I wanted. For one, I didn't love the oil and gas industry, and second, the positions I held did not align well with my personal mission and vision. I have always been an avid reader and a sponge for new knowledge, and my ultimate goal was to use this knowledge to help others. My vision for my own personal career was thus one that achieved this mission in a comprehensive way. In one way or another, I knew I wanted to have a career that allowed me to reach thousands of people and share with them ways to enhance their lives.

I set several goals for myself in an effort to achieve the career I wanted. Some of my first goals involved acquiring the tools necessary for such a career. I defined goals to read several personal growth and self-empowerment books for two hours every day. I challenged myself to complete courses that taught me how to be a dynamic speaker within a period of two years. And I began to develop my own message and method for empowering others through the Quality Core Process. Each of these goals was measurable, imaginative, challenging, achievable, realistic, and explicit. At the same time, as I moved closer toward attaining each goal, I became more excited about the possibility of my new career. Each goal was also structured so that one supported another at just the right time.

By developing these goals, I was able to measure my progress toward the dream career I wanted and better attain my own personal career mission and vision. They served to hold me accountable along the way, and they also helped motivate me and push me forward in my efforts to advance. No matter what your dream job or career may be, create goals that help you stay focused and dedicated in your efforts. Change is often difficult, but having an effective road map to help you adapt in a step-by-step way over time makes things simpler and easier. Take the time to create these goals, and you will reap the benefits as a result.

Step 3 – Take an Inventory of Your Current Situation

The third step in the QCP involves an analysis to help you determine where you are in achieving your goals and the level of quality you desire. When it comes to your job or career, this requires making some assessment of your current position, your current skills, as well as an overall evaluation of where you are in your potential career path. Why is this important? Because this is an essential step in determining what strategies and pursuits you will need to take to attain your dream job. If you are unclear about your current situation, it is nearly impossible to determine the next steps to take in achieving your short- and long-term goals.

Let's start with your current status in your career or position at work. Is your current job aligned with a path that will naturally help you attain your ultimate career goals? If you are a restaurant manager who ultimately wants to own your own restaurant, then certainly your current position can help you one day accomplish your goal. But what if you wanted to open your own fitness training gym and become an exercise expert? While you may gain important managerial experience and knowledge of healthy nutrition, your current position at the restaurant is unlikely to naturally move you in that direction. Depending on this initial assessment, you can immediately appreciate the magnitude of the changes that may be needed in your strategies to pursue a higher-quality career.

Next, you need to take an inventory of the skills and talents you will need to effectively perform in your future career. What educational requirements are typically needed to attain such a position? Is a certain level of experience required? If so, how can you get this experience? What obstacles are in your way in attaining these abilities? Do you have any unique opportunities or contacts that would help you acquire these skills? Every job has a unique set of requirements, and likewise, every individual has a unique set of abilities and opportunities. You simply need to evaluate how your unique situation and the specific requirements of your dream job "match up." In doing so, you will be better able to see the gaps that require your attention.

Essentially, this part of the QCP involves performing your own SWOT analysis as it relates to your career. List your strengths and weaknesses in relation to your dream job, and then examine opportunities as well as barriers (threats) that might affect your ability in achieving the career you desire. Strengths and weaknesses typically involve things like education, job experiences, specific areas of expertise, specific physical or mental talents, and other personal attributes. In contrast, opportunities and barriers involve things outside of your control like finances, time availability, social obligations, personal contacts, job offerings, and more. All of these areas are important in determining where you will need to focus your efforts in your future pursuit of the career you seek.

The last aspect of the analysis step requires an assessment of where you currently exist in your career trajectory. Let's assume you have determined your career goal is to be your own boss and open your own investment consulting firm. What challenges might you face if you were twenty-five years old? What if you were forty years of age? How about fifty-five years old? In each instance, different circumstances may dictate unique considerations in the development of your ideal strategy to attain that career. The recent college graduate who has only delivered pizzas part time will need a different strategy than the middle-aged manager who has worked in the financial industry all of her life. Likewise, this same middle-age manager might pursue a different timeline when compared to someone more advanced in age in the same position.

While this part of the analysis is important, it should not serve to discourage anyone from pursuing the dream job they desire. Certain life situations may make it more difficult and challenging to attain the career you want, but that career is not necessarily unattainable. The QCP does not identify which career pursuits you should take based on the level of difficulty required to make the change ... it only helps you see the path to get there. Regardless of whether this path is a piece of cake or approaches the impossible, ultimately it will be you who determines if the path is worth taking. In other words, only you can define what represents quality in your career and the degree of effort you are willing to take to achieve that quality.

Step 4 – Develop (and Act On!) Strategies for Your Career Master Plan

At this point of the QCP, you have done a lot of work toward pursuing your ultimate career. You have defined your dream job, established measures to evaluate your progress toward that goal, and assessed your current situation. It's now time to create targeted strategies to close the gap and realize that quality of work life you deserve. Unfortunately, many people may get this far in the QCP and fail to take the next step. Even worse, they may even create some effective strategies but never pull the trigger and act on them. Inertia is often the biggest deterrent when it comes to making your dream career a reality.

Developing effective strategies for the job you desire can be broken down into four categories that align with the analysis you performed in Step 3 of the Quality Core Process. These categories involve revisiting your strengths, your weaknesses, your career opportunities, and the things that threaten you from achieving them. Additional aspects of strategy will involve timing and sequencing, but these will be discussed last. To start, you should create strategies based on these four main areas in order to maximize your chances for success.

Let's start with your strengths. At first glance, you might assume you don't need a strategy related to your strengths because, after all, they are strengths! But this is not necessarily true. Consider the heart surgeon who has become an expert at removing blockages from the coronary arteries by performing a bypass graft operation. Given that this is a wonderful strength he possesses, his practice flourishes. He sees little need to change things as a result. But within a few years, the preferred treatment for blocked arteries shifts from bypass grafts to artery stents placed by a catheter. Despite having the same skill set, the surgeon suddenly finds he is losing patients to other heart doctors who are able to perform the new procedure. Because he failed to consider his primary strength in an ongoing strategy for his career success, his career takes a step backward.

In today's world, change is constant and fast. In developing a set of career strategies, do not forget to consider your current strengths. Strengths must be continuously renewed and often enhanced in order to maintain a competitive edge in the job market you seek. You might be an excellent manager practicing the best management techniques today, but if you fail to continuously maintain these skills, you may soon find other managers with knowledge of the latest trends in leadership leapfrogging you for the position you wanted. The question to ask yourself is, "How can I make sure my talents at _____ continue to be top notch in the years to come?" The answer might involve continuing education, new experiences, or many other choices, but the important thing is to ask the question. Maintaining and enhancing your strengths need to be a part of your career strategies.

Next, develop strategies to help overcome any weaknesses you might have in attaining the career you desire. As mentioned, I realized that I needed not only additional knowledge in order to pursue the career I wanted, but I also needed specific skills. While educating myself through reading helped overcome many of these weaknesses,

I also took several courses and workshops to enhance my abilities in speaking and motivating. What is the best strategy for you to address your weaknesses? How can you best go about closing the gap between your current knowledge, abilities, and experiences and those required by your dream job?

Numerous options exist in helping you overcome any shortcomings, and it will be up to you to determine which ones are best for your own personal situation. In some cases, formal education might be the best strategy. In others, additional personal or professional experiences might be required. For example, a friend of mine leveraged his current strengths in healthcare to change careers and become a professional writer. Formal education in journalism or English was not required in order for him to pursue this new career, but he still needed new skills and insights. So, he pursued these needs through a series of part-time projects that allowed him to write about health. Being imaginative in setting goals is important, as is being creative in developing strategies to overcome existing limitations.

Having considered strategies to enhance your own personal strengths and overcome your weaknesses, examining which strategies can seize available career opportunities is your next consideration. The key component in this phase is to be proactive and to avoid complacency. The worst thing you can do is fail to act. You don't want to find yourself filled with regret about a missed opportunity that you ignored. If you have identified an opportunity to realize your dream career, or at least move in that direction, develop strategies to make the most of it. If opportunity is knocking on the right door at the right time, you certainly need to answer the call.

Many strategies are useful to enhance your opportunities for career success. One of the most important involves extending your number of personal and professional contacts. Networking is essential in today's world of competitive careers. It *is* about who you know as much as it is about what you know. Consider strategies to market yourself and your talents to others. Be sure they know your career aspirations. In fact, others can often help you formulate strategies to further you along toward your goals. Ask questions, promote yourself, express interests, and stay alert to subtle opportunities.

The last category related to career strategy formation involves minimizing barriers and threats to your success. Many of these challenges are beyond your control. For example, the job you want may require significant investments in time and/or money that you may not have available. Perhaps the job openings at existing companies for your desired position are limited. Or maybe your field of interest is changing so rapidly that predicting the best position for your career down the road is nearly impossible. In each of these instances, you can and should create strategies to reduce these obstacles as best as possible.

Once again, creativity and imaginative thinking can be your friend in developing strategies to minimize risks and barriers. Let's assume you lack the finances to return to school and gain additional degrees. Naturally, student loans and leveraging your existing assets may offer traditional strategies in overcoming these obstacles. But other possibilities might also exist. Corporate internship programs, educational grants, and unconventional scholarships might exist to help you attain the needed credentials for your career advancement. Truly out-of-the-box thinking might involve presenting your own "package" to your company to help you meet mutual goals and objectives. The same applies to a highly competitive field with limited job openings. Perhaps your best strategy might be to launch your own business as a means to attain the position you want. Never give up, never give in . . . create the quality career you deserve.

A few final comments about developing your career strategies:

- First, strategies work best when they can be constructed in a step-by-step fashion. In other words, create strategies for each accomplishment required along the career path you have defined. While "end-result" strategies are important, so are the ones that keep you moving forward.

- Second, everyone's timeline varies depending on their circumstances. Different stages of a person's career and the desired career trajectory influence how quickly you choose to reach specific milestones. Align your strategies with these timelines in mind so you can create practical and successful approaches to attaining your dream career.

Step 5 – Step Back and Reassess

As is always the case in the QCP, anything you don't frequently revisit has the potential to undermine all your efforts made in the preceding steps. Consider the following story:

A midlevel software engineer at a reputable firm set his sights on becoming the company's chief information officer within the next ten years. Methodically, as many engineers might do, he defined his goals, analyzed his situation, and developed strategies to place him in a favorable position to realize his dream. Over the next ten years, he pursued additional college degrees, gained several industry-specific certifications, and volunteered for many relevant company projects. He immersed himself in these tasks to such an extent that he failed to realize the company had eliminated the position altogether in favor of using a consulting firm. Unfortunately, while all of his efforts had been valuable, he still lacked experience as a chief information officer and could not attain the position elsewhere.

In this case, we again have a clear forest and trees problem. Initially, the young software engineer effectively assessed the company landscape and his ultimate career goal (the forest). But after developing specific strategies to attain that position at the company, he became too fixated on the tasks involved (the trees). Where did he go wrong? He never reassessed whether or not his strategies were helping him realize his ultimate goal of being a chief information officer. Once he was in the trees, he never came back out to see how the forest had changed.

In almost every industry and career, things are in a constant state of flux. Some are naturally more dynamic than others, so constant reassessment and reevaluation is necessary. This not only applies to the strategies you employ, but to every aspect of the Quality Core Process. Do you still desire the career and job you initially wanted? Have your mission, vision, values, or goals changed? Do the measurements and goals accurately measure progress toward your career goals? Do the strategies you are pursuing align well with the ultimate plan? Ask these questions and others on a regular basis so you are not caught off guard like our young software engineer. While the trees are certainly important, every now and then you have to step back and make sure the forest hasn't changed in the process.

In trying to figure out when you should reassess your plans, goals, and strategies, several variables come into play. If your industry or market is rapidly changing, then these reassessments should occur more frequently. If your timeline for advancement or change is brief, you should likewise reassess your progress constantly. And if you're experiencing constant setbacks or unexpected results, this again requires more frequent reevaluations. The goal is to reassess often enough so you can appreciate progress, since this provides motivation and encouragement. But at the same time, you should not wait too long so that some or all of your efforts are wasted on unproductive strategies. In time, determining how often you should reassess will become more intuitive as it relates to your specific situation. But in the meantime, erring on the side of more frequent rather than less frequent is likely prudent.

In generations past, a person would most commonly pursue a single career in their lifetime. Today, this is no longer the case. In fact, many individuals today seek more than one career at a time, and changing careers at different life stages is certainly not uncommon. Regardless of the situation in which you may find yourself, the QCP can be effectively used to help you identify and pursue the career (or careers) of your dreams. With our occupations representing such a significant part of our lives, a quality career can enhance the quality of our lives. By applying the QCP to this important area of your life, you will be better positioned to enjoy enhanced quality in other areas of your life as well.

Chapter 4

Quality Core for Your Health

At some point in your life, you have likely had a bad case of the flu. Suddenly, every muscle and joint in your body aches, your head throbs with intense pain, and you constantly negotiate your every move since any abrupt change could send you running to the restroom. In that misery that seems to float between living and dying, you mourn the loss of well-being that you had a few days earlier. You begin to bargain for a better outcome. "If I ever get over this, I promise to take better care of myself." But eventually, you do get better, and those promises made during the darkest hours of the illness tend to carry less influence on your daily behaviors. We've all been there . . . that's just human nature.

Things can become a little more complex in other situations. What if you have some type of long-standing health problem rather than a temporary case of the flu? Maybe you suffer from severe arthritis and joint pain. Perhaps you have had some type of injury or trauma that has left you disabled. Or maybe you have some progressive condition that limits your length of life. In these instances, opportunities for recovery and improvement are not nearly as likely, and somehow you must come to terms with your poor health condition. Of course, how you respond can vary significantly. This reaction can have a tremendous impact on your ultimate quality of life above and beyond the specific limitations your illness has imposed on you. Here again, you seek ways to gain the best quality of life you can, given the cards you have been dealt.

Overall, four major categories affect a person's quality of life. These aspects include a person's income, their attitude, their environment, and their health. As we have discussed, your career can be a major determinant of your quality of life. This naturally impacts your income, your immediate environment, and perhaps even your attitude. But health is another major determinant of your life's quality. In fact, some estimates suggest health may be the most important factor in how you perceive your overall well-being.[10] Thus, considering measures to promote better health makes perfect sense when it comes to your overall quality of life.

Step 1 – How Do You Define Health?

You have likely heard the phrase, "If you have your health, you have everything." In considering this statement, I am reminded of one of the lessons I learned early in life when taking tests in school. Whenever

---

10 Laura Landro, "The simple idea that is transforming healthcare," *Wall Street Journal*, 2013, https://www.wsj.com/articles/SB10001424052702304450004577275911370551798.

presented with a true-false question that contains "never" or "always," the answer is almost always "false" (notice I said "almost always!"). So, your health may not provide everything you need for a quality life. Other variables play a role as well, but without question, health is one of the major factors involved. In addition, how you define health can determine its role in influencing your overall quality of life.

Consider the following example. A young woman goes swimming in a nearby lake with her friends. While playing on a zipline that they came across, the line suddenly breaks, causing her to fall in the lake and strike her leg on some rocks, suffering a large gash. After receiving care at the emergency room and getting several stitches, she is sent home. But within hours, her left leg becomes black with intense pain. Over the course of the next several weeks, doctors struggle to keep her alive, and eventually she loses portions of all her limbs. Given this scenario, you would likely assume the woman would describe her health as poor. You might also assume she'd perceive her quality of life as negative. But you would be wrong.

The woman is Aimee Copeland. Her unexpected encounter with a flesh-eating bacteria was both rare and profound. But today, she would not describe her quality of life as poor. In fact, she often describes her trauma as being life changing and positive, leading her in directions she could never have imagined. While she would love to be able to walk again, the opportunities her condition has offered her has enhanced her overall quality of life. As a result, she is an inspiration to thousands of people and describes herself as happy and content.[11] You might not have expected this to be her response given the health conditions she has suffered.

Let's consider another example. A young male athlete is recognized as a tennis prodigy, and over time, he advances to become one of the best tennis players in the world. He exercises daily, practices his tennis skills incessantly, and adheres to a strict diet designed to maximize his performance on the court. He wins match after match and ultimately becomes one of the greatest tennis players of all time. On the surface, most would say he was in perfect health and presumably had "everything." But how would he describe his own quality of life? Very poor. He had played tennis for years while hating the sport deeply, and over time, it progressively sucked the happiness out of his life. His name was Andre Agassi.[12]

What explains the different views of quality of life in these two examples? In one, quality of life was noted to be high despite suffering a loss of limbs, while in the other, quality of life was poor despite being in perfect health. At first glance, you might question whether health truly influences quality of life to a significant degree. But in examining these cases in more detail, you can appreciate the

---

11 Jason Hanna, "Aimee Copeland would do it all over again," CNN.com, 2016, http://www.cnn.com/2016/10/28/health/aimee-copeland/index.html.
12 Matt Bromigan, "10 pro athletes who really hate their jobs," TheRichest.com, 2015, http://www.therichest.com/rich-list/10-pro-athletes-who-really-hate-their-jobs/.

differences based on how health is defined. If we simply define health as physical well-being, then Aimee's and Andre's quality of life outcomes make little sense. But if we expand our definition of health to include mental, social, spiritual, and emotional areas of well-being, then we can better understand their outcomes.

The growth Aimee Copeland experienced emotionally and spiritually greatly enhanced her overall perspective of well-being despite the pain, loss of physical abilities, and other problems. For Andre Agassi, loneliness and depression significantly undermined his capacity for a quality life despite being one of the premier athletes in the world. How you define health is critically important in determining its effect on your life's quality. Health should be viewed as much more than just physical wellness, and the scope of its definition determines what goals and strategies you ultimately pursue in an effort to have a high-quality life.

Though a holistic view of health is preferable, each area of health is weighed differently for every person. Some individuals relate quality of life to physical health while others give greater value to emotional and spiritual health. For others, mental health is associated with a high-quality life, especially if they may have suffered from various mental health problems in the past. How you define good health determines which aspects of health influence the quality of your life the most.

So, how can you best define health as it pertains to your own life? The best approach is to consider health from multiple perspectives, or more accurately, from a holistic perspective. Evaluate all five areas of health, including physical, emotional, mental, social, and spiritual. By assessing how you define health in each of these categories, you will gain a better appreciation of your overall view of health and the importance each of these areas offers in promoting wellness. The following offers a guide in trying to determine how you define health as it relates to quality in your life:

- Physical health – How important is physical function and well-being to you? What role does exercise play in your life? What level of physical function is needed for you to be happy? What aspects of physical health are most important (being pain-free, driving, exercise, sexual activity, good sleep, etc.)?

- Emotional health – How important are your mood and feelings in providing a quality life? What impact do your mood and feelings have on your daily ability to function? How much do your mood and feelings affect other areas of health (mental, social, physical)?

- Mental health – How much is your ability to think, remember, and pay attention linked to your well-being? What role do your mental abilities play in your daily life, your career, and your social interactions?

- Social health – How important is it to you to have a wide network of friends and close relationships with family? Do you fear isolation or loneliness? What impact do good relationships have on your mood, your attitude, and your motivations?
- Spiritual health – How important is spirituality or religion to you and your well-being? Does your spiritual health offset poor health in other areas? To what degree does spiritual health impact your overall quality of life?

As you can see, each of these areas of health is interrelated. Emotional well-being can improve mental and physical functioning, and spirituality might offer enhancements to the quality of your life despite having poor mental health or physical illness. Regardless, how you answer these questions (and others relevant to these areas of health) affects how you define health overall. Therefore, considering your definition of health by examining its multiple dimensions can provide you with better clarity about the health goals you need for a high-quality life.

Step 2 – Set Your Health Goals and Targets

Once you have defined what health means to you and how it can potentially impact your quality of life, you will likely want to make some changes. Taking this first step can certainly be enough to motivate you in this direction. After all, the diet industry has benefited greatly from low levels of "beginner motivation" for centuries. In fact, more than half of the people who diet and initially lose weight end up weighing more than they did at the start within a few years.[13] So, how can you pursue real health without losing motivation and persistence?

Overall, the QCP helps you in this regard. Setting effective goals to attain health is an important part of this process. Like career goals for a higher-quality life, health goals should also exhibit the same characteristics. They should be measurable, imaginative, challenging, achievable, realistic, exciting, explicit, and timely. Likewise, they should also be incremental, allowing each goal attained to support the next one. By setting goals and measures of health in this fashion, you will be able to sustain motivation, enthusiasm, and commitment to a much greater degree. Often, efforts at dieting fail because the initial goals established were either overzealous or lacked the capacity to sustain their pursuit.

Suppose you want to get serious about your physical health, so you decide to run a marathon. Being a real go-getter, you set your goal to run the marathon within the next two months. You start running after work and on weekends, and before you know it, the date of the race is upon you. Equipped with the latest running fashion and hi-tech shoes, you confidently begin the race, but somewhere around

---

13 Stuart Wolpert, "Dieting does not work, UCLA researchers report," UCLA Newsroom, 2007, http:// newsroom.ucla.edu/releases/Dieting-Does-Not-Work-UCLA-Researchers-7832.

mile nine or ten, you know you aren't going to finish. If the feelings of failing aren't enough to discourage you from future attempts, the profound soreness in every muscle of your body over the next week certainly is. So, you put the shoes and running attire in the back of your closet and surrender to your pre-marathon lifestyle.

In this scenario, your goal was certainly challenging, explicit, measurable, imaginative, and exciting. But unfortunately, it was not realistic, achievable, or timely. As a result, the initial motivation to improve your health dissipated as you experienced setbacks. Even the most seasoned runners appreciate the importance of setting goals with these attributes when considering a marathon. The distance they run each week is increased gradually and incrementally over a long period of time to maintain their motivation and enthusiasm. They will often run with other individuals training for marathons, or select new trails or paths on which to run to sustain their excitement. And their little successes along the way help them to keep a positive attitude and motivation for the ultimate goal.

Determine health goals for both the short term and the long term. Pursuing good health, regardless of your definition, is certainly more like a marathon than a sprint. Your goals may evolve and change over time, as they do in other areas, but you should always maintain a long-term perspective in your efforts to establish effective health goals. And as described in the last section, each defined area of health (physical, emotional, mental, social, and spiritual) should receive your attention in this regard. The following table can provide a framework for you in identifying key goals in each area:

Health Definition Category	Health Goals Considerations
Physical health	• Exercise and activity goals – athletics, group activities, strength training, aerobic activities • Diet and nutrition goals – daily calories, weight, food types, micronutrients • Sleep goals – daily and weekly amount, schedules
Emotional health	• Stress management goals – relaxation techniques, guided imagery, isolation time • Emotional expression goals – journaling, partner communication time
Mental health	• Memory exercise goals – word games, puzzles, structured cognitive tasks • Reading and academic educational goals – self-educational activities, formal educational activities, personal growth activities
Social health	• Social activity goals – group activities, community events • Personal relationship goals – partner relationships, family relationships, friend relationships • Professional relationship goals – work colleagues, work acquaintances
Spiritual health	• Spiritual practice goals – meditation, prayer, religious services • Spiritual educational goals – spiritual readings, spiritual lectures • Spiritual activities – volunteer services, charity activities

In many instances, goals that you create can serve more than one health need. For example, charitable activities can serve not only spiritual needs but also social and stress management needs. Likewise, you may identify one category of health as being much more important to your quality of life than others. In this case, you would create specific goals within that particular category in your pursuit of a higher quality of life and health. By using the categories of health as a guiding framework, you can create effective goals using the techniques described in this section. These goals can then serve as targets for strategies that facilitate your ability to attain better health and a better quality of life.

Step 3 – Identify Obstacles and Opportunities for Better Health

The next step in the QCP is analyzing your current health status. For health, the "A" in the DMASR process requires more than simply assessing gaps between your current level of health and the goals you have set. It also involves examining barriers that could keep you from attaining these goals since you will likely need specific strategies to overcome these obstacles. At the same time, you will also need to identify unique opportunities that will allow you to achieve these health goals with the least amount of effort and energy. This part is particularly important when it comes to maintaining health, since setbacks and "backsliding" are common.

Not long ago, I found myself in a less than ideal health position. In 2016, I decided to run for congressional office, and naturally, this endeavor required an abundance of my time. Not only did I have less time to exercise and take proper care of myself, but I also began eating foods that provided both a quick calorie fix as well as a bit of comfort. Nothing says "good job" for a long, hard day like a nice, hot slice of pizza! By the time the campaign was over, I had gained sixteen pounds. It was time for some health quality control, so I reexamined my situation as well as my goals so I could adopt a better approach in regaining my health. I realized rather quickly that the current demands on my time, and the level of stress associated with running for political office, had undermined my normal health routines. By identifying these health barriers, I was able to focus on areas that needed the most attention.

How do you go about identifying health barriers and opportunities? I have found the best way is to examine these areas from both intrinsic and extrinsic perspectives. In other words, these barriers and opportunities can originate within us or outside of us. Let's take some examples. Suppose you live in a busy, inner city area. This location could impose barriers to health if your environment prevents you from having areas for physical activity. At the same time, you might have easy access to public transportation that offers other health opportunities. These would be examples of extrinsic (or external) factors that influence health goals and strategies.

Now suppose you also suffered from chronic pain and depression. The associated lack of energy and motivation could result in intrinsic barriers to health. You might be less motivated to act on specific health strategies and pursue specific health goals because of this. At the same time, you might have excellent physical abilities that enable you to exercise and improve your mood. This would be a potential opportunity to enhance your health through intrinsic (or internal) attributes. When examining health barriers and opportunities, consider both extrinsic and intrinsic areas.

In evaluating extrinsic factors related to your health situation, three major areas are typically involved. These include economic factors, sociocultural factors, and environmental factors.

- <u>Economic factors</u> – income level, health insurance coverage, food prices, local costs of living
- <u>Sociocultural factors</u> – trends in exercise, trends in diets, trends in social activities, cultural preferences in diet, cultural spiritual practices, beliefs regarding health, family dynamics, social status
- <u>Environmental factors</u> – access to physical activity, access to healthy foods, access to transportation, community health

services, access to social activities, access to spiritual and religious activities

The items within each extrinsic category are not meant to be exhaustive, and you will likely identify additional barriers and opportunities in pursuing your health goals in each category as it pertains to your unique situation. Regardless, the framework does help you in considering some of the more common external factors that affect your ability to attain higher quality health so you can structure health strategies accordingly.

In contrast, identifying intrinsic barriers and opportunities to attaining your health goals can be a bit more challenging. For example, someone with a depressed mood and chronic fatigue may fail to realize the impact this has on their ability to pursue healthy activities. Or one may not recognize high levels of emotional stress despite undermining one's health goals related to better sleep and spirituality. Despite the difficulty recognizing intrinsic barriers and opportunities for better health, these factors do align well with the specific categories of holistic health in most cases. The following offers a framework for assessing these specific intrinsic barriers and opportunities:

- Physical factors – pain, energy level, endurance, mobility, balance abilities

- Emotional factors – mood, attitude, patience, tolerance, enthusiasm, motivation
- Mental factors – stress level, attention capacity, determination, rationalization abilities, education level
- Social factors – friend support, family support, work support, relationship motivations, social needs
- Spiritual factors – spiritual convictions, spiritual motivations, spiritual supports, life experiences

As you may notice, the intrinsic factors listed (like the extrinsic ones) do not indicate their tendency to be a barrier or an opportunity in relation to your health goals per se. Instead, this framework simply provides some features of each category that might encourage or discourage your ability to attain the health you deserve. Once you have identified these factors, you are then ready to create specific strategies to overcome barriers and to take advantage of opportunities that align with your health goals.

Step 4 – Health Strategies for Success

In this part of a normal quality control process, businesses and organizations will typically look at their strengths, weaknesses, opportunities, and threats in an effort to devise strategies to maximize their success. Likewise, they will leverage positive factors against negative ones while striving to develop competitive advantages against other companies in the market. Extrapolating these approaches to your health, the QCP offers some similarities in strategy development. After all, like businesses, you have a limited number of resources (time, money, energy, etc.), and you need to use them well in order to attain your health goals as best as possible.

In Step 4, four considerations can help you create effective health strategies in pursuing a high-quality life. The first consideration involves the importance of the health goals you have identified. Which health goals are a priority right now? Which ones are a priority long term? Is your mental health more important than your physical health at the moment? Or are you looking to achieve complete, holistic health from the start? In order to establish the strategies that will result in true quality health for you, you must assign priorities to each of the major categories of health (physical, emotional, mental, social, and spiritual). In addition, developing a list of priorities for each of the goals within each category will also be important. In this way, you can allocate your time and energy in developing strategies toward those goals first.

The second recommendation in creating health strategies involves identifying those that can meet more than one goal at a time. Consider this example. Suppose you want to exercise three times a week, be more socially outgoing, and at the same time develop a deeper sense of spiritual awareness. One option might be to join a fitness club at your local church. In this instance, one strategy has served to meet several health goals. Some health strategies are mutually reinforcing in their ability to attain your goals as well. For instance, exercise often helps you lose weight while also suppressing appetite, so if you also have weight-loss goals, this strategy may inherently move you further toward your ultimate health vision.

Next, leverage any activities you do, or opportunities you have, to help achieve your health goals. By creating health strategies in this fashion, you exert less effort and use fewer resources in the process of pursuing better health. For example, one of my health goals after my political campaign was to lose the weight I had gained. But at the same time, I also wanted to enhance my spiritual well-being and foster a positive attitude. After reading Tim Ferriss's blogs and watching some of his podcasts, I adopted several of his strategies that linked my physical, spiritual, and emotional health. While each of the strategies was different for each health goal, I used one resource opportunity (Tim Ferriss) in defining specific health strategies. As a result, I wasted less time in strategy formation and in acting on those strategies.

The final consideration in developing health strategies to achieve your goals relates to timing. Short-term goals provide more achievable results while providing continued motivation and encouragement. Long term goals, however, ultimately move you toward a higher quality of life as it relates to your health. Based on these considerations, you want to develop strategies to help you accomplish each step (short-term goal) as you continually move forward. And likewise, long-term strategies should complement these shorter ones, and vice versa. Use your strategies to help you remain focused and on task, and to remove potential obstacles as well.

Perhaps it should go without saying, but I will say it again anyway . . . strategies are of no use unless you act on them. After spending time and effort on defining quality health, setting goals, assessing barriers and opportunities, and developing well-aligned strategies, it would be a shame to let all of this go to waste by failing to pull the trigger. If you have performed the preceding steps of the QCP well, acting on your health strategies will serve you in two ways. Naturally, they will provide positive feedback as you achieve better health quality. But at the same time, simply participating in these activities will provide excitement, enthusiasm and motivation. Use action to fuel your persistence, and in time, your continued successes will perpetuate your ongoing pursuits.

Step 5 – Examine Your Health Report Card

Remember getting those midsemester report cards in school? At some point in the term, you would receive an update on your current grades in your classes. Many times, I wish I had gotten to the mailbox before my parents when those reports were mailed. The reports served an important purpose . . . they gave you a head's-up in time to make some changes before the semester was over. This last step of the QCP in relation to your health encourages you to "check in" regularly to see how you are progressing so similar changes can be made if needed.

The last step in the DMASR is "R," which stands for reevaluation, but it could just as easily be listed as "A" for accountability. Accountability can be difficult when you are the only person involved. My young daughter probably would not attempt to "steal" a cookie before dinner if I were standing in the kitchen. Why? Because she would be held accountable for her actions in some way. But if I were not there, the chance exists that she might get away with the petty crime. And if she did, no one would be there to hold her accountable for her actions except her own conscience. Of course, that might be enough to prompt her to confess or even refrain from taking the cookie. But at the same time, that divine, sweet taste of the cookie might be enough to convince her otherwise.

Reevaluation provides an opportunity for you to be held accountable for your goals, strategies, and actions in pursuing a healthier life. If you are not getting the results you predicted, then any of these may need to be revised. Were your goals realistic, achievable, and explicit? Do they motivative and excite you? Do the strategies you created help you attain your goals, or do you need to come up with a different approach? Have you acted on the strategies you created? If not, are there other barriers you failed to see along the way? Depending on the answers to these questions, various parts of your quality control plans may need revisions.

During this step of the process, you might realize you need a little help in the accountability department. If so, enlist others to help you. If some of your priority goals involve greater social activities and enhanced social health, this might be a perfect opportunity for you to improve your health strategies at the same time. Join groups with similar goals and strategies so other people can help keep you on track and motivated. Recruit friends and family members to oversee your efforts to encourage your level of commitment. Sometimes during the reevaluation step, you may find a complete overhaul of your goals and strategies are not needed. Instead, you might just need a little oversight and support to nudge you along the way toward your ultimate health goals.

As you reassess your progress in moving toward your health goals, try to be as objective as possible. Failure is not anything to be ashamed of when striving for a higher quality level of health. In fact, failure is simply an opportunity to refine your QCP to make it more effective and successful over time. Even the best QCP application can change over time. Even if your initial strategies and efforts were making great progress, you may find things change in time that cause you to stall out or regress. For this reason, the reevaluation phase of the QCP is a necessity, and it must be performed often and regularly. Like many things in life, health is not static. It is constantly changing. Reevaluation allows you to "tweak" your plan to keep up with these changes while getting the most out of your efforts.

Having your health may not mean you have everything, but the impact your health has on your quality of life is undeniable. This is particularly true when you consider health from a truly holistic perspective, as described in this chapter. By including social and spiritual health along with physical, emotional, and mental health targets, you will be more likely to address key areas in your life where gaps can be filled and quality of life improved. By following the same QCP (although specifically tailored to health concepts in this chapter), you can outline a plan to attain health quality in both the short term and long term. And by putting in the effort and time to define, measure, analyze, strategize, and reevaluate your overall health quality, your opportunities to realize a high-quality healthy life will grow dramatically.

Chapter 5

Quality Core in Your Finances

So far, we have talked about how to apply the QCP to your career pursuits and to your health. As you might suspect, these applications should be placed in the particular priority most applicable to you. For most, a successful career means little if poor health limits their quality of life. But at the same time, career may be a priority if your health is currently good and you have healthy habits. With that said, one of the common areas in which many of us struggle for quality in our lives relates to how we manage our financial affairs. It only makes sense to consider how we can enhance our quality of life through better money management. After all, who wouldn't like to have the added security of being financially stable?

If you think you need a little help with your finances and budgeting skills, you are not alone. Did you know that nearly eight out of every ten people live paycheck to paycheck?[14] In fact, a quarter of people who make salaries over $100,000 a year do so. This coincides

---

14 Aimee Picchi, "Vast number of Americans live paycheck to paycheck," CBS News, 2017, https://www.cbsnews.com/news/americans-living-paycheck-to-paycheck/.

with the fact that about a third of people have less than $1,000 in savings at any given time.[15] Of course, living paycheck to paycheck as a philosophy of life may be perfectly fine. But evaluating your philosophy about spending and saving allows you to make sure your actions align well with what you see as a quality life. And believe it or not, how you spend your money can tell you a lot about your overall priorities in general!

In this chapter, we will explore how you spend and save your money as well as the changes you might like to make. Just as prior chapters have applied the QCP to specific areas of your life, this chapter will do so as well. But along the way, some guides and insights about money management will be provided to help you determine the strategies that work best for you and your financial goals. Thus, we'll apply the same DMASR framework but with a unique spin in relation to spending and saving behaviors. If you are one of the many who struggle with budgeting, then this chapter will provide you with some excellent ideas and insights about how to enhance the quality of your life in this specific area.

---

15 Matthew Frankel, "20 money stats that will blow you away," The Motley Fool, 2016, https://www.fool.com/investing/general/2016/02/01/20-money-stats-that-will-blow-you-away.aspx.

Step 1 – Define the Ideal Budget for You

When you're trying to create a budget, where do you start? Most people start by determining their basics. In other words, what are those things you can't live without? This is certainly not a bad place to start. After all, we all need housing, clothes, transportation, and food. It only makes sense that we start with our basic needs. But here is where it gets a little tricky. What is a need, and what is, well, not? Is that pair of designer shoes you bought on sale last week truly a need simply because it falls in a category of clothing? Some of you might say "Yes!" rather emphatically. Does a new luxury SUV fall in the category of a need? Perhaps if you have five children and a job that demands a certain lifestyle appearance, it very well may.

The bottom line is that only you can determine what is truly a "need" versus a "want" as it pertains to your life. What might be a necessity for someone might be a luxury for someone else. To help you in defining your needs, we can provide some basic strategies. With each expenditure you consider, ask yourself the following questions: "What would happen if I did not have this item or service in my life? Would its absence significantly impact my life in a major way?" If the answers are yes, then it is likely a need. If not, then it may simply be a want.

Let's consider a friend of mine who recently divorced and moved out on his own. Divorce can naturally be rather costly, so he was trying to re-budget in order to get a handle on his finances. As he went through his bills and expenses, he pondered whether cable television was a necessity or not. What would you say? My friend decided it was not, so he went without it. Over the next few months, he found he read more books, listened to more music, and streamed more television programs and shows, but he didn't notice any loss in his quality of life. For him, cable television was not found to be a need.

Defining needs in your life relates to those things that are important in order to have a reasonable quality of life. They reflect the essentials required for you to be comfortable and content. These will naturally vary from person to person. But when defining your basic needs, be sure to keep things simple. What are the basics you need to get by on? The reason this is important relates to the formula you will apply to your spending versus your saving behaviors. Needs require expenditures while wants typically do not. If everything is a need, then your ability to save and budget might be significantly compromised. But if you define your needs based on the things that are true necessities, then you will be better able to implement an effective quality control process in your budgeting.

Let's consider another example. You would likely agree that clothing is a necessity when it comes to your spending. Even nudists have to wear clothes some of the time! But to what extent are your clothes a true need? Consider the man who purchases a suit from a discount outlet store. If he is required to wear a suit for his job, then the purchase is likely an expenditure based on need. But if he already has dozens of suits in his closet and simply purchases the suit because it is on sale, then it would be hard to make the case that it is a true need. Sometimes, these distinctions can be difficult to make, but taking the time to highly scrutinize needs versus wants will help you better define your spending priorities.

Having established the importance of defining needs and wants, the next question then becomes how much should be spent on needs versus wants. Here again, you will need to consider your own specific situation, but as common formulas suggest, we should spend 50 percent of our take-home income on necessities while only 30 percent on the things we want.[16] Keep in mind, the 30 percent of your income for the things you want does not pertain simply to things like vacations, spa massages, and eating at fancy restaurants. These certainly fall into the "want" category. But any "upgrades" you choose to purchase in clothing, cars, foods, and other necessity items also apply to this category. Once you factor in these upgrades, you can appreciate the fact that this 30 percent of your income can be spent fairly quickly.

If half your income is spent on needs and 30 percent on wants, where does the remaining 20 percent go? You probably guessed it . . . savings. While most people save less than 5 percent of their income,

---

16 Elizabeth Warren and Amelia Warren Tyagi, *All Your Worth: The Ultimate Lifetime Money Plan* (New York: Simon and Schuster, 2005).

most experts encourage a savings rate around 20 percent.[17] On a positive note, however, this savings rate includes debt repayments. For example, you may use 10 percent of your income for the payment of credit card balances and car loans while saving or investing the additional 10 percent. If you have no debt, then you might apply the entire 20 percent to your savings and investments. Regardless of what you decide is best for you, defining how you are going to distribute your spending and saving on a regular basis establishes the foundation for a higher-quality outcome.

Step 2 – Measure the Value in Your Spending

You have probably heard the adage, "Put your money where your mouth is." In most cases, the saying challenges someone to back up what they are saying with action. But it also highlights another important point . . . we tend to spend money on the things we most value, whether consciously or unconsciously. When you spend money on products or services you know that you need or want, you act in a conscious manner. But at other times, purchases might be more impulsive, sporadic, and based on unconscious whims. It might be only the next day (or later that month when the credit card bill arrives!) that you begin to realize the repercussions of your actions.

---

17 Ibid.

Take the guy who occasionally travels to Las Vegas for a weekend with "the boys." From a conscious perspective, he plans the vacation and sets aside a portion of his income for his flight, hotel room, and rental car. Likewise, he knows he will be gambling some, so he also reserves a couple of hundred dollars for his entertainment. But once he arrives at the casinos, he becomes enthralled with the blackjack tables. Before he realizes it, he has taken out several hundred dollars more on his credit card so he can continue to enjoy himself (and hopefully win back some of his losses!). Did he receive any value for his additional spending? In terms of entertainment, probably so. But the spending was not necessarily conscious or planned; instead, it was impulsive. And after he returns home, he may very well wish he had made a different decision.

As you can imagine, credit card companies rely on these moments when you choose to spend impulsively. Each of us has the ability to make strong excuses for such actions. "I have a work bonus coming up at the end of the quarter, so I can afford this now on my credit card." "In the long run, spending this now will save me money later." "I should make this purchase on my credit card because I get reward points." The potential for rationalizations are endless, but in each case, we justify debt spending outside of our budget for things we want (and do not necessarily need). What's the underlying problem? The failure to define the value received for each expenditure made.

Fortunately, several tools exist to help you with identifying options for credit cards and loans. Spending the extra time to research and investigate different options is essential in assessing value. For example, some credit cards have significant annual fees while others do not. Some have outrageous interest rates. Then there are "payday"-type loans that charge extreme rates and fees. These are almost never a good idea. Websites and other financial instruments on the Internet allow you to compare and contrast different credit options, and taking an hour or so to investigate this information could literally save you thousands later.

Let me make one thing clear . . . I am not saying that all credit card spending is unconscious or impulsive. Certainly, many circumstances occur where credit cards are needed to meet an immediate need. Life is life, and emergencies and unpredictable situations occur that may demand the use of credit cards to meet a true necessity. However, in other instances, credit cards are used to satisfy wants consciously or unconsciously, and in the process, our long-term quality of life is affected when it comes to our financial well-being. This is why it is important to consider a thing called value-based budgeting, which is a key part of the "Step 2 Measurement" aspect of the Quality Core Process.

What is value-based budgeting? In essence, this system requires you to determine your spending priorities based on your actual values ahead of time rather than determining how to spend your money "on the fly." What are the things you value the most? Health is likely one area that you value, but do you set aside money for quality health insurance? You also likely value your relationships, but do your spending and saving patterns reflect this? Perhaps you value travel. Do you set aside enough savings to ensure you can travel regularly now or have a retirement plan to do this later? If you answered yes to these questions, then you are likely practicing value-based budgeting. But if your saving and spending habits fail to reflect the things you value the most, then it may be time to reassess.

In order to measure your current quality-of-life situation related to your financial well-being, perform two interrelated activities. First, start with making a list of your priority value items. The following table represents a list of common areas where value and spending should coincide. Feel free to add more, but this activity requires you to rank categories from highest to lowest based on the value you assign to each. This will give you some idea about your priorities when it comes to value spending.

Spending Category	Priority Value Ranking
Home and utilities	
Transportation	
Health and well-being	
Family vacations	
Retirement savings	
Clothing	
Food – Groceries	
Food – Dining out	
Personal care	
Entertainment	
Debt repayment	
Education and career training	
Charity donations and gifts	

Now that you have completed this activity, let's move on to a second one. You will use the same table that you used for the first activity, but this time you will determine the categories in which you spent the most money. Instead of putting your money where your mouth is (which in essence pertains to the first activity), you will be seeing where your money has been going. Go back at least three months, or preferably a year, and rank the categories again based on your actual spending patterns. You can do this by placing each of your expenses in a specific category (like housing, groceries, car expenses, entertainment, etc.) and then dividing the amount of each category by your total after-tax income. This will let you see the percentage you spend in each category listed. This will provide an excellent way to see where current spending and saving behaviors can be improved.

Spending Category	Actual Spending Behavior Ranking
Home and utilities	
Transportation	
Health and well-being	
Family vacations	
Retirement savings	
Clothing	
Food – Groceries	
Food – Dining out	
Personal care	
Entertainment	
Debt repayment	
Education and career training	
Charity donations and gifts	

After performing these exercises, you will be able to identify any gaps that may exist between your ideal spending preferences and your actual spending behaviors. With this information, you can develop specific goals so these gaps are eliminated. Perhaps you spend too much on your car and too little on family vacations. Maybe room for improvement exists in the amount spent on dining out, your education and training, or your retirement investments. Or you might find your spending matches your priorities and values quite well. Regardless, these two activities serve to provide a measurement of your current spending and saving as it relates to your values, and this can be done repeatedly over time to revisit your financial quality of life.

As a final note regarding this step of the QCP, keep in mind the recommended percentages of your income that should be used on necessities, wants, and savings. You certainly do not have to align your spending and saving behaviors with these recommended percentages, but you should develop your own percentages to use as a regular guide. In addition, when filling out the tables, keep in mind the discussion about needs and wants. For example, you may have housing as a priority value, but the money spent on housing as a necessity versus that spent on housing upgrades may undermine your ability to have a true value-based budgeting plan (Step 4). Being aware of this now will help you better analyze and strategize throughout the Quality Core Process.

Step 3 – Take the Deep Approach to Analysis

In applying the QCP to the financial aspects of your life, the initial two steps have provided you with a great deal of information. You have now defined needs and wants as well as your own personal values in spending and saving. You also have a pretty good idea about gaps and discrepancies between your current spending habits and the ones you would prefer to have. Now, it is time to figure out the underlying issues that caused these gaps in the first place. For instance, you might spend too much on dining out at restaurants and too little on retirement, but *why* do you choose to do this? In other words, what makes you spend money in ways that is against the things you value the most?

The analysis step in the QCP can be rather challenging since it requires you to dig a little deeper than you might typically. As a result, this step of the process in relation to your finances is not only highly individualized but also quite personal. You might realize the reason you dine out so frequently is because you lack confidence in the kitchen. Or maybe you dine out because you are isolated during your working hours and need social interaction. Thus, while you value your health and future savings, you constantly undermine these spending behaviors in an effort to satisfy other basic human needs. For this reason, the analysis step is particularly important when it comes to your spending and saving patterns.

Consider the following scenario. A couple was recently married, and they decided to start a family. Much to their surprise, their doctor announced they would be parents of twins. Not only did this mean extra financial burdens for the couple, but it also meant the wife would need to quit her job for a period of time, given the extra responsibilities. The immediate solution was for the husband to work additional hours in order to make ends meet, which seemed to work well initially. But over the next year or so, their budget changed significantly. While the husband's additional income was enough to cover the basic needs of the family, it wasn't enough to pay for the rise in credit card spending. Before they knew it, they were spending a significant portion of their budget on debt repayments.

Why did things take such a turn for the worse? After all, the additional income was enough to meet their initial financial needs. However, the wife suddenly found herself immersed in the care of two infants while temporarily having to give up her career. Her career, which was associated with her own self-esteem and happiness, had been put on the back burner, and she progressively had become saddened and depressed. In an effort to soothe these unwanted feelings, she began purchasing various goods and service that temporarily gave her some small amount of pleasure. Of course, these purchases were above and beyond the couple's normal spending budget, and it eventually undermined their other financial values.

Getting to the root of the problem is often difficult. In many instances, the measurement step in the QCP identifies *where* your spending or saving has gone awry, but the analysis step explores the reasons *why* this has happened. As you might imagine, understanding the "why" is important because it provides the basis for strategy development in the next step. For instance, you might appreciate that you save too little for your retirement, and you may even commit to saving more. But unless you appreciate the actual reasons behind your incongruent behaviors, the chance you will repeatedly fail in sticking to your commitment is fairly high.

There are many ways to explore the deeper reasons you spend and save the way you do. Self-reflection, talking with close friends, and even therapy may offer some useful insights about your financial habits. But one approach examines your basic human needs in relation to your spending patterns. Maslow's hierarchy of needs may offer a framework through which you can explore the reasons you spend and save the way you do. The following is a graphical depiction of Maslow's hierarchy.[18]

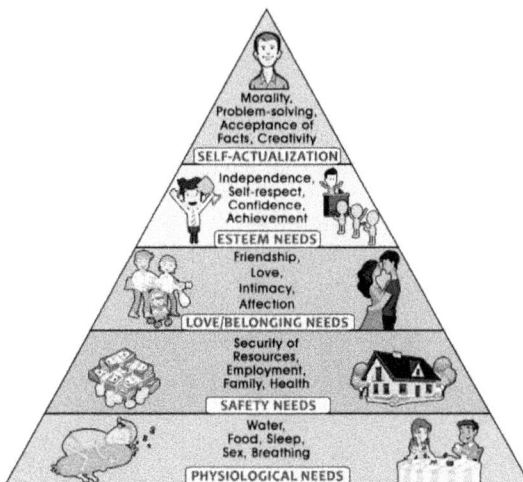

Morality,
Problem-solving,
Acceptance of
Facts, Creativity
SELF-ACTUALIZATION

Independence,
Self-respect,
Confidence,
Achievement
ESTEEM NEEDS

Friendship,
Love,
Intimacy,
Affection
LOVE/BELONGING NEEDS

Security of
Resources,
Employment,
Family, Health
SAFETY NEEDS

Water,
Food, Sleep,
Sex, Breathing
PHYSIOLOGICAL NEEDS

---

18 Andy Gibbons, "Maslow's hierarchy of needs and motivation of teams," LinkedIn.com, 2016, https://www.linkedin.com/pulse/maslows-hierarchy-needs-motivation-teams-andy-gibbins.

If we examine Maslow's pyramid, the needs at the lower level are the most essential ones, with each level higher representing needs that can only be addressed effectively once lower-level needs have been met. Returning to our example, we can see the wife (and couple) initially had some safety needs related to financial resources after they found out they were having twins. But once the husband addressed these needs, higher-level needs involving self-esteem and achievement took center stage for the wife. The inability to constructively resolve this level of needs eventually led to some unwanted spending habits.

Using Maslow's hierarchy of needs as a framework for analysis may not be the best approach for you, but it might reveal some key reasons why your spending and saving is not well aligned with your desires. Regardless of how you approach the analysis step of the QCP as it relates to your financial behaviors, try to define the rationale behind your spending patterns. If you can get to the basic motivations, then you will be much more likely to develop effective strategies to get your budget back on track.

Step 4 – Strategy Formation: Looking Near and Far

At this point, you know how you would like to spend your money. You also know where discrepancies are between your ideal budget and your actual spending and saving behaviors. And you hopefully have a good understanding why these discrepancies exist. As a result, you are now ready to develop some strategies to get you headed in the right direction. But what strategies are most effective? How can you devise a plan of action that keeps you on track? To answer these questions, it is important to again keep in mind needs, wants, and values. These ultimately will help you be more effective in attaining your quality financial goals.

We have already talked about value-based budgeting. Now, we are going to talk about value-based strategies. Having identified the list of priorities for your ideal spending, use this list to create an effective budget strategy. Make sure those items at the top of your list receive your financial attention first. For example, if you value a solid retirement plan the most and want to put aside 20 percent of your income for retirement investments, then this needs to be paid before anything else. This is a value-based strategy . . . those things of the greatest value and priority are addressed first followed by items of lesser value and importance.

Having said this, do not forget about the results of your deeper analysis. Let's say you want to save 20 percent of your income for retirement, and you pay this out of your paycheck first. Understandably, you likely place needs like housing, food, and transportation above this priority, but perhaps you failed to consider the level of importance regarding your health. As a result, you choose to forego health insurance and the gym membership to save more for retirement.

This might be ideal for you, but what if you develop some type of chronic illness several years down the road? You might have ample funds in your retirement account, but your health may prevent you from enjoying retirement the way you had imagined.

This example is not to show specific areas of spending that should be a priority, but it is meant to highlight the importance of keeping your strategic focus on long-term perspectives in addition to the immediate future. Developing strategies for a quality-centric financial plan can be complex and challenging because of this dual focus. You have to balance short-term values and needs against long-term ones. Both are important, and neglecting one over the other can result in a less than desirable outcome. You may choose to use the prior tables from Step 2 listing your priorities to define short-term and long-term preferences separately. Once this is done, you can then integrate these tables in a manner that feels right to you for specific budgeting strategies. Regardless of your approach to strategy formation, keeping your eye on short- and long-range targets is key.

Step 5 – Take a Fresh Look . . . Over and Over Again

The last step of the QCP is naturally reassessment. For finances, this is not only an essential step to make sure strategies are effective, but likewise, it is important because both financial priorities and climates change frequently. Life throws you curves on a regular basis, and what might have been a financial priority before may no longer be at the top of the list. Changes in your job, your health, your family, and your relationships can affect your values, as can many other life experiences. Likewise, interest rates, housing markets, and other changes in the economic climate can also influence priorities.

The frequency with which you choose to reassess your financial strategies and priorities naturally depends on your life situation. If you are experiencing many changes on a regular basis, then you should reassess your spending and saving habits often. Likewise, if prior reassessments have shown repeated shortcomings in attaining your goals, reevaluations should occur more regularly until you achieve some degree of success and stability. When it comes to your finances, perform reassessments often. Even though strategies for long-term goals may be difficult to assess when performing frequent reevaluations, the ability to assess whether short-term goals are being attained still provides excellent insights.

In terms of practicalities, using the prior values and spending tables allows you to examine whether or not continued gaps exist between your ideal spending and your actual behaviors. Likewise, by comparing past tables from current ones, you will be able to assess whether you are making progress or improvement. If you repeatedly fail to make progress toward your financial goals, then repeat the entire QCP once again. Not uncommonly, changes occur that undermine your original strategies and plans, and these can be better identified by repeating the entire QCP step by step. This can also help you to identify reasons for your lack of success that you might not have realized previously.

Money cannot necessarily buy you happiness, but it may affect the quality of your life. Therefore, managing your money and finances well is important, and the QCP offers a method by which you can better align your personal values with how you spend and save. Each of the steps of the QCP is important when it comes to improving your spending because each step builds on the preceding ones. In order to develop effective financial strategies, effective analysis is required. And effective analysis demands insights about your current spending patterns, your values, and your ideals.

The same process to achieve quality control in your spending and saving can help you attain short-term and long-term financial success as it relates to your perspectives and values. Putting the QCP to work for you to improve your financial well-being is certainly a task worth pursuing.

Chapter 6

Quality Core and Your Relationships

In ranking how important quality is in different areas of life, where do you rank relationships? Does fortune or fame rise to the top of the list? Perhaps a successful career is most important to you. Interestingly, a survey of millennials recently showed four out of every five listed "getting rich" as the most important quality-of-life indicator, and half cited "being famous" as ranking near the top of the list.[19] In many societies throughout the world, these aspirations are linked to quality of life, at least in terms of common societal perspectives. But research shows these areas are much less important compared to our relationships.[20]

The Harvard Study of Adult Development has been cited as the longest known study of human health. The study, which began in the 1930s, enrolled over seven hundred men and followed their lives for over seventy-five years through serial interviews, medical examinations, and tests. One group of men was initially sophomores

19 Robert Waldinger, "What makes a good life? Lessons from the longest study on happiness," TED Talks, 2015, https://www.ted.com/speakers/robert_waldinger.
20 Ibid.

at Harvard University, while the second group consisted of poor, disadvantaged boys living in Boston. The researchers reached two major conclusions. First, good relationships were the only consistent predictor of happiness and health among all the participants. Second, loneliness and social isolation were linked to poor health and reduced length of life. The study also found that the quality of one's relationships were a much more important predictor of health and longevity over the number of relationships. This study shows how important our relationships are to our well-being.[21]

Therefore, it seems prudent to apply the QCP to our own personal relationships in an effort to attain a higher-quality life. Many of us struggle with relationships, whether with a significant other or with our coworkers. At some level, all of our relationships have the potential to impact the quality of our lives, whether positive or negative. The goal is to maximize the positive effects while minimizing the negative ones, and through a quality control process, we can do just that. Though the same QCP will be discussed once again, the specific steps described in each of the sections will provide a unique focus of their application to our personal relationships. As a result, you will better understand the level of quality each of your relationships provides for you personally as well as steps you can take to improve them.

Step 1 – Define a Quality Relationship

21 Ibid.

You have likely heard divorce statistics quoted fairly routinely throughout your life. According to the American Psychological Association, 90 percent of people have married by the time they reach fifty years of age. But at the same time, 40 to 50 percent of these couples will divorce. And if you track the divorce rate for second marriages, the percentage is even higher.[22] Do these figures mean that only half of all individuals who marry enjoy a quality relationship? Not necessarily.

Because of the negative connotations associated with divorce, whether religious or social, some people choose to stay in a marriage despite having a poor-quality relationship. In fact, some marital relationships are quite toxic, leading to higher risks for physical and mental health conditions.[23] At the same time, many divorced individuals end up having good relationships with their ex-spouse. Such couples are not well suited to be married but are able to enjoy a positive relationship as friends that add value to their lives.

So, what exactly defines quality in a relationship? One way to define a good quality versus a bad quality relationship is to examine the effect it has on your life. Does the relationship empower you, make you smile, energize you, or challenge you in some sort of positive way? Do you look forward to seeing the other person, spending time with them, and interacting with them? On the other hand, do

---

22 American Psychological Association, "Marriage and Divorce," APA Website, 2017, http://www.apa.org/topics/divorce/.
23 Waldinger, 2015.

you tend to avoid seeing the other person, make excuses or cancel meetings, or "dilute" your interactions with them by having others around? Do you get anxious, nervous, or depressed in anticipation of interacting with them?

One of the best yardsticks in defining the quality of a relationship is to examine how it makes you act and feel. High-quality relationships make you feel good and promote positive behaviors, while poor-quality relationships often do the opposite. In other words, the proof is in the pudding. If it's made from a good recipe with fresh ingredients, the pudding will probably taste pretty good. And if not, it might leave a pretty sour taste in your mouth.

After you have defined the current quality of your relationships based on their effect, next define the level of intimacy that each relationship offers. You might immediately assume intimacy means some type of passionate, loving exchange with another person. While it may, intimacy is better defined as the depth of the relationship and its level of personal closeness. For example, you can have a profound, intimate relationship with a lifelong friend or a family member. Intimacy does not imply any type of sexual attraction or closeness. Instead, it describes the degree with which you allow yourself to be vulnerable and real in a relationship. The more intimate the relationship, the deeper the connection.[24]

24 Matthew Kelly, *The Seven Levels of Intimacy: The Art of Loving and the Joy of Being Loved* (New York: Simon and Schuster, 2005).

Matthew Kelly has outlined seven levels of relationship intimacy from superficial to deep.[25]

- Level 1 – Clichés. Here, the relationship operates on a superficial level that might be best described as chit-chat. Think about daily interactions with sales clerks and cashiers.

- Level 2 – Facts. This level is characterized by sharing basic facts about yourself, like your occupation, marital status, and place of birth. Think about interactions you might have with someone you just met at a restaurant while seated at the bar.

- Level 3 – Opinions. At this level of intimacy, some opinions are voiced between two people. While still relatively impersonal, some revelations about preferences and beliefs might be conveyed. Think about interactions you might have when attending a book club or meet-up group.

- Level 4 – Hopes and Dreams. Level 4 intimacy relationships begin to open the door to the expression of personal aspirations. Some work relationships or those with people who you see regularly commonly operate at this level of intimacy.

- Level 5 – Feelings. Sharing your emotions and feelings about various subjects reveals deeper qualities about yourself. Where opinions are thoughts based on facts and beliefs, emotions

25 Ibid.

are more personal in nature. Casual friendships might be an example of this level of intimacy.

- <u>Level 6 – Fears, Faults, and Failures</u>. At this relationship level, one expresses vulnerabilities with a presumed willingness to accept the weaknesses of others. A variety of close relationships may enjoy this level of intimacy, including those with close friends, family members, and significant others.

- <u>Level 7 – Deep, Legitimate Needs</u>. This is the highest level of intimacy where one seeks to be truly known and to know the other person. This commonly involves relationships with significant others but may also involve friends and family members, depending on the depth of the relationship.

A few clarifications need to be mentioned when defining your relationships' intimacy levels. First, relationships rarely operate at only one level. Most of the time, your relationships span a few levels, so when evaluating each relationship, try to define its level of intimacy based on its most frequent intimacy level. Second, a neat progression from a lower level of intimacy to a higher one does not always occur or even need to occur. A casual encounter may quickly jump to a high level of intimacy, while long-term relationships, including marriages, may never reach the highest levels of intimacy. Appreciating these two caveats will help you better define the intimacy levels of the important relationships in your life.

The final step in defining your relationships involves your innate sense of the importance each one has. For example, you may not have the strongest marriage in the world, but this relationship may be your top priority. Perhaps the relationship with your children or your parents has a high level of priority in your mind. This part of Step 1 is simply your assessment of how important various relationships are in relation to your quality of life. Once you have defined your relationships in terms of priority, intimacy, and effect, you will then be ready to move onto Step 2 of the Quality Core Process.

Step 2 – Measure Current Relationship Quality

Positive effects and higher levels of intimacy have been shown to produce better physical and mental health.[26] Step 2 involves measuring the quality of each of your relationships to determine where you can make improvements.

The following table offers one way to measure the current quality of your existing relationships by compiling the information gathered in Step 1 and calculating the cumulative effect on your relationships. For each of the relationships you consider, fill out the following table according to life effects, intimacy levels, and priority rankings. For life effects, lower scores are considered negative while higher ones are more positive. Rank each relationship's effects on a scale of one to

---

26 Waldinger, 2015.

five accordingly. Then, simply list the intimacy level most commonly encountered with each relationship. This would be scored from one to seven according to Kelly's levels of intimacy.[27] Last, rank these relationships from one to five based on their importance to you intuitively. Lower scores imply lesser importance than higher scores.

	Relationship 1	Relationship 2	Relationship 3	Relationship 4	Relationship 5
Life Effect (1–5)					
Intimacy Level (1–7)					
Priority Rank (1–5)					
Total Score (Range 3–17)					

*Life Effect – 1=highly negative effect; 3=neutral effect; 5=highly positive effect

*Intimacy Level – 1 through 7 based on most common intimacy level interactions

*Priority Rank – 1=low priority; 5=high priority

Once you have filled out these parts of the table above, simply add the three subcategory scores to obtain the total score for each relationship. The relationships with the highest scores will be those

27 Kelly, 2005.

that currently have the most positive and influential impact on your life's quality, while those with lower scores have lesser benefits. For example, let's assume your marriage has a score of 15 while your relationship with one of your parents is 7. Based on that total score, your marital relationship is currently having a more positive impact on your life's quality than your relationship with your parent. This same information can be used to examine which relationships are currently having the least beneficial impact on your quality of life.

How do your relationship scores look to you? Were they what you expected? If some of the total scores seem low, or even if all the scores are on the low side, this is no reason to get discouraged or make broad assumptions about the relationships in your life. Some people, for example, have few intimate relationships, while others may have several. Likewise, the magnitude of the impact any relationship has on your life may be less when compared to another person. The importance of this exercise is to simply see where room for improvement might exist. After all, that is the main objective of the QCP . . . to find areas where continuous quality improvement can occur.

Step 3 – Analyze Any Relationship Shortcomings

Without question, relationships can make your life rich and fulfilling. At the same time, however, they can also cause stress and worry.

When things are going well, you feel on top of the world, and when they are not, you want to crawl in bed and hide. Most of my life, I have been fortunate to have wonderful and strong relationships that have helped support me during good times and bad. But everyone has negative relationship experiences at times. Relationships are meant to challenge us and cause us to reexamine ourselves and our lives. Through them we grow personally and sometimes even spiritually, and this ultimately enhances the quality of our lives in many ways.

When I decided to leave my family's oil and gas business to explore new career opportunities, my decision created some strife and conflict in my relationships with my family. In fact, at times we did not speak for several weeks as a result of disagreements and different perspectives. While it is true that relationships require both sides to make an effort toward improvements, a great deal can be gained through our own personal actions.

With this in mind, the third step of the QCP involves analysis of your relationship abilities and skills. Analyzing your talents in this area does not imply you are necessarily at fault or that you are the reason a relationship is going poorly. In fact, it may be time for some relationships to go on their own merry way while cutting your losses. But through analysis, you can learn how to improve many relationships that are struggling while enhancing those that are on solid ground. All of us can benefit from better relationship skills, and this is a great area for you to consider for quality improvement.

In deciding which relationships you wish to analyze first, the choice is yours. Those with higher total scores are naturally doing better than others, and these may not require your immediate attention. However, at the same time, their inherent level of priority may encourage you to examine them in greater detail regardless. Where you start is less important than the number of relationships you analyze. The more positive, high-quality relationships you can create, the better your quality of life will likely be.

In analyzing each of your relationships, you will examine five different attributes. Each of these will provide you with opportunities to improve the relationship quality depending on which areas appear to be the weakest. After the analysis is complete, you may determine the relationship is not worth the amount of effort required in comparison to the benefit it might provide. That's OK. Sometimes a relationship is simply too toxic to be salvaged or too far gone to influence your life in a positive way. However, most of the time, the analysis step highlights the potential your relationships have for being a positive force in your life and areas where improvements can be made.

The analysis step involves five areas of assessment. These include the following:

- <u>Self-reflection</u>. Do I have a personal agenda? Am I competing with the other person in some way? What behaviors do I exhibit that provoke conflicts and disagreements? Am I close-minded or resistant to change?
- <u>Communication skills</u>. Do I actively and patiently listen? Do I express my real feelings and thoughts in a genuine way? Do I allow the person time to express before commenting or interrupting?
- <u>Emotional intelligence</u>. Do I effectively empathize with the other person and their situation? Do I have a good idea how they feel about the relationship, about specific circumstances, and about their view of life? Do I take the time to consider their feelings and reactions?
- <u>Authenticity</u>. Am I real, honest, and genuine in my interactions with the other person? Do I give my undivided attention to them when they are speaking and expressing? Do I share my own faults and weaknesses with the other person? If not, do I feel safe in doing so?
- <u>Commitment level</u>. What amount of energy do I invest in this relationship? How much time do I devote to this relationship each day, week, or month? Does this relationship take precedence over other activities? If not, which activities seem more important and why?

By asking yourself these important questions within these five categories of analysis, you will have a good understanding about areas where improvements in a relationship might occur. For example, you may realize that you are constantly "one-upping" the other person by sharing your own experiences that seem more noteworthy than theirs. This pattern can be changed through personal improvements in self-reflection and through enhanced listening skills. Perhaps you have simply neglected to spend time with a person or consider their emotions or perspectives. These can be improved by making changes to your schedule or through asking how they feel about specific topics. While strategies will be discussed in the next step of the QCP, this analysis of your relationships provides the information needed upon which to develop these approaches.

Step 4 – Targeted Strategies to Build Better Relationships

Have you ever met the guy who seems to mesh well with everyone he meets? You know the guy . . . within a few minutes, he has engaged in a deep and meaningful conversation with someone he just met, exchanges contact information before he leaves, and follows up not by phone but in person for coffee a few days later. Everyone with whom he encounters seems to quickly bond with him at a fairly deep level, and over time, his social network of relationships becomes enormous. Not only does he have dozens of relationships, but each one is fulfilling, meaningful, and rewarding. How does he do it?

Let's face it, some people are just naturally talented in developing strong relationships with others. Their social skills are superb, and likewise, they are caring, genuine, interested, unselfish, and engaged with others they meet. But each of us can learn the majority of these abilities and skills. Depending on the areas you have identified in your relationships that need work, you can select various strategies to help overcome these shortcomings. The following strategies are common ones to help you improve areas where you may struggle in your relationships. The list is not comprehensive by any means, but it does offer some proven strategies to improve the quality of your relationships.

- <u>Schedule the time</u>. Nothing says you care quite like the time you spend with someone. Examine your schedule and see where you can arrange to spend more time with the person with whom you are in the relationship. Be flexible and accommodating as best as possible. Once you start making concessions to ensure you are spending time with them, they will often do the same. This is a necessity for the relationships where you identified a low commitment level, but it can also help any relationship regardless of the issues.

- Focus the time. Spending time is important, but this time can be of little use if you are constantly distracted during the encounter. Smartphones, tablets, and other devices are common attention-stealers today, but noisy and highly stimulating settings can also be distracting. If you are making time to spend on a relationship, make sure it is quality time free of interruptions and distractions. This strategy can enhance areas of commitment, communication skills, and authenticity.

- Be real, honest, and genuine. Stronger relationships tend to reach deeper levels of intimacy, and in order to achieve this, you must be real, genuine, and honest. This approach may be challenging and scary. It can provoke conflict at times while also making you feel vulnerable. However, if you truly want a higher-quality relationship, this strategy is important. Naturally, this strategy is beneficial for relationships lacking authenticity, but it is also useful in advancing communication abilities.

- Improve your listening skills. Communication in a relationship is a two-way street. Unfortunately, we often get wrapped up in telling our side of the story and venting our own frustrations without considering the other person's perspectives and problems. If you want to improve your relationships, learn to actively and patiently listen to others. You will learn much more about them in the process, gain their trust and respect, and better understand how they feel about specific issues. This can enhance relationships where communication, emotional intelligence, and authenticity are poor.

- <u>Improve your expression skills</u>. Expressing yourself in a general way may not be as big of a challenge as listening, but expressing yourself deeply can be. Deep and meaningful expressions require you to be vulnerable and revealing, and this can provoke fear and concern. Cautiously experiment with what you express and with whom you do, but through the process, you should gain confidence in sharing yourself with others. This can greatly help relationships where authenticity is lacking and where better communication is needed.

- <u>Develop empathy.</u> The ability to have emotional intelligence and empathy comes easier for some than others. However, everyone has the capacity to enhance their skills in these areas. Begin by taking the time to ask yourself what emotions the other person is experiencing. Then, test your gut feelings by asking the person how they feel. In time, you will not only improve your general skills for empathy, but you will also become better at knowing how that individual feels. In addition to helping relationships with poor emotional connection, this strategy also improves authenticity and communication.

- Invest in self-reflection. Spending more time interacting with others is important, but taking the time to self-reflect is also critical. Use this time to examine if you have any specific agendas, biases, or areas of judgment. Or use it to identify specific weaknesses, vulnerabilities, and concerns. In the process, you will be more aware of the areas where you need to improve your relationship skills, and you will have a better idea how various relationships are affecting you.

- Get help. While all the strategies described above can help you greatly improve your own relationship skills and strengthen existing relationships in your life, sometimes professional help may be required. Psychologists, marriage counselors, relationship counselors, and other therapists can evaluate key aspects of a relationship and offer insights and strategies to facilitate improvements. If pride or other obstacles are in the way, do your best to remove them. Before giving up on a high-priority relationship, enlisting a professional can be quite helpful regardless of whether it reinforces termination of the relationship or places you back on the right path.

- Just say yes! – Relationships are important to everyone, but not everyone has wonderful social skills. Some people tend to be more introverted while others may be shy or fear being awkward. If relationships are important to you for enhancing quality in your life, then putting yourself "out there" is a must. Too many times we say "no" instead of "yes" and miss a great opportunity for attracting positive relationships in our lives.

The strategies cited in this section can provide you with a number of approaches to enhance the quality of your current and future relationships. Of course, you may not pursue all of these strategies. Select those that you think would be helpful for a specific relationship, and then attempt these specific ones. As always, resources (especially time) are limited, and choosing relationship strategies wisely is important. By using the QCP, you are better able to select which strategies might be most effective based on your prior relationship analyses.

Step 5 – Reevaluate Your Relationships Time after Time

Most of the life areas to which we have applied the QCP are dynamic and constantly changing. This is particularly true for relationships. How we interact with others can vary significantly depending on changes in our lives, their lives, and a number of other circumstances. In addition, how each individual in the relationship reacts to the various strategies used in Step 4 also affects whether the relationship improves, worsens, or stagnates. Perhaps more than the other life areas discussed in this book, the reassessment step of the QCP is important when it comes to your relationships.

There is another reason why reassessment of a relationship's quality is important. As noted at the beginning of the chapter, relationships (more than fortune and fame) have a profound impact on our health and longevity.[28] If your ultimate goal is to enhance your overall quality of life, then relationships should be a priority among the areas where you might apply the Quality Core Process. On average, the better high-quality relationships you have, the healthier you will be. And with better health, your career pursuits (and possibly your ability to meet your financial goals) are better supported.

One final word about relationship reassessments. Like other areas, the frequency with which you reevaluate a relationship will vary depending on its priority and its need for improvement. For example, your marriage might be at the top of the list if you value it highly and are having a number of issues. By using the measurement table in this chapter, you will be better able to determine which relationships need more frequent reassessments and which ones can be reevaluated less often. However, only you can determine when reassessment is required. Your level of commitment, investment, and concern regarding a specific relationship will drive the frequency with which to reexamine progress. There is no set, specific timetable for reevaluation.

By applying the QCP in regard to your relationships over and over again, you will be able to see if your strategies and analysis are

---

28 Waldinger, 2015.

effective and accurate. It is always possible that nothing you try will enhance a relationship's quality. After all, both parties must make mutual effort to realize true improvement, and in some cases, you may even fail to make any progress despite effort being made on both sides. If this happens, the QCP offers value here as well. By repeatedly examining the quality of your relationships, you can see what works, what doesn't, and when it may simply be time to let a relationship go. All of these outcomes can have positive impacts on the quality of your life when evaluated correctly.

Chapter 7

Applying Quality Core to Your Thinking

In the preceding chapters, we have applied the QCP to a number of more concrete areas of your life. But what about positive thinking? Certainly, you can make an effort to improve your perspective and outlook on life, and this will improve the "quality" of your thoughts. But will such an endeavor improve the quality of your life? Absolutely!

You don't have to take my word for this. Over the last couple of decades, science has supported the simple fact that more positive thinking leads to better health and better personal outcomes. Over seventy thousand women were studied at Harvard's College of Public Health, and the top quarter of optimistic thinkers were 30 percent less likely to die from cancer, heart disease, stroke, respiratory disease, or infection when compared to the lowest quarter of the sample.[29]

Positive thinking has also been shown to help those with various mental health conditions like depression and anxiety. In fact, a common type of mental health therapy (cognitive behavioral therapy)

29 Karen Feldscher, "How power of positive thinking works," *The Harvard Gazette*, 2016, http://news.harvard.edu/gazette/story/2016/12/optistic-women-live-longer-are-healthier/.

seeks to educate individuals and change their understanding so they can then change their behaviors. This occurs because they have a shift in perception.[30] A logical next step is to apply the QCP to your thinking patterns to strive for a higher-quality life.

In this chapter, the QCP will be used to help you define, measure, analyze, strategize, and reevaluate your degree of positive thinking in your life. The chapter will also explore the relationship between positive thinking and quality. The more positive thinking you do does not necessarily equate to higher quality in all instances. Like everything, too much of a good thing can be detrimental. Positive thinking without reality checks can lead you down an unproductive and unhealthy path, and blind, positive faith without awareness and insight can do the same. As a result, the use of positive thinking in the QCP encourages logical and practical approaches to enhance your life's quality without taking you over the edge.

Step 1 – Understand Positive and Negative Thinking

Have you ever had to speak publicly in front of a large crowd of people? I have. I can still remember the first time I had to give a speech in front of an audience. I was absolutely terrified. My hands were trembling, my heart racing, and small beads of sweat broke out on my forehead. I am not sure whose voice started to come out of my mouth at the

---

30 Barbara L. Frederickson, "Updated thinking on positivity ratios, *American Psychologist* 68, no. 9 (2013): 814–818.

beginning of the speech, but it certainly didn't sound like mine. Like most people with whom I have talked since that time, I had a less than optimal experience during my first public speaking opportunity. In fact, public speaking routinely ranks among Americans' greatest fears (even above death in some cases!). Fortunately, my negative experience was not repeated over and over again.

Over time, I became much more adept at public speaking. I even ran for the US House of Representatives, and now I confidently speak to crowds all the time. But how did I get from that anxious, fearful person to a confident, adept communicator? Certainly, experience and practice helped, but the mindset I had going into each speech evolved over time. The thoughts in my head during my first few speeches were much different than those later in life. Thoughts of failure and embarrassment were eventually replaced with thoughts of confidence and purpose. While these were not the entire reason for my improved public speaking abilities, they did have a significant influence.

Positive thoughts are those associated with positive emotions and outcomes. Examples of positive thoughts might include, "I will do well on this examination," "I am well-prepared for this presentation," or "By being honest, I know things will work out for the best." Positive thoughts can include affirmations about yourself or an expectation that things will go well. They typically evoke feelings of well-being, confidence, and happiness. And they naturally focus on a higher level of quality in your life.

In contrast, positive thinking can be defined by what it is not. It does not involve negative thoughts and emotions. Negativity anticipates the worst outcomes and expects things to go less well than they should. Negative thinking also undermines self-confidence and self-esteem by being critical of your ability to perform or succeed. Examples of negative thoughts might include, "I should have studied more," "There is no way I will get that promotion," or "Things are going too well, so I know something bad is about to happen." Just as positive thinking evokes positive emotions, negativity evokes feelings of fear, anxiousness, and worry. Sometimes the best way to tell if your thoughts are positive or negative is by taking note of how you feel.

In this first step, you should simply gain an understanding of what thoughts can be considered positive and which ones negative. Some thoughts are best considered neutral. That's perfectly fine. You can even influence your neutral thoughts to enhance quality in your life. Overall, defining your thoughts as positive or negative is relatively straightforward. By examining the expectations each thought assumes, and by evaluating the feelings triggered by these thoughts, you can usually categorize them as positive, negative, or neutral.

Step 2 – Take an Inventory of Your Thoughts

Barbara Fredrickson is a social psychologist who has dedicated her career to examining positive psychology. She has conducted a number of research studies related to positive thinking and health. In performing these experiments, she developed instruments that allow her to quantify the number of positive and negative thoughts a person has over the course of days or weeks. Interestingly, she has found that a positivity ratio (the number of positive thoughts per day compared to negative ones) of about 3 to 1 provides the greatest advantages to one's health.[31] In other words, having more positive thoughts than negative ones enhances your quality of life.

In applying the QCP to this area of your life, you must measure the degree of positive and negative thinking that you have. As we noted in Step 1 in defining positive and negative thinking, your thoughts are naturally linked to your feelings. Therefore, one way of measuring your level of positive thinking can be performed by assessing your emotions throughout the day. Fredrickson offers an online instrument in this regard that provides you with a positivity score, a negativity score, and a positivity ratio.[32] Your target goal is to have a positivity ratio of 3 to 1.

31 Barbara Fredrickson, *Positivity* (New York: Three Rivers Press, 2009).
32 Barbara Fredrickson, "Positivity self-test," PositivityRatio.com, 2009, http://www.positivityratio.com/single.php.

Fredrickson's approach has you examine your feelings to determine how positive your thinking is. At the same time, you can also examine your actual thoughts and expectations. This may be more challenging since it requires frequent sampling of your thoughts throughout the day or week to gain an accurate measurement of your thinking patterns. Likewise, these samples must be performed at regular intervals and over a reasonable period of time to help ensure a true inventory of your thoughts. You might decide to sample your thoughts every half hour, every hour, or less often; however, the less frequent the sampling time, the longer you will need to assess your thinking behaviors.

You can use the following scorecard to track your thoughts and your overall thinking behavior. The time interval should be consistent and simply listed in order from the first to last time sample. The positive-negative rating should be on a scale from +3 (very positive) to -3 (very negative), with 0 being a neutral thought pattern. Your total score is then simply a summation of the rating values.

Time Interval	Positive-Negative Rating
Total Score	

In assessing your total score in this exercise, a measurement that is positive will support positive thinking patterns, while a negative score does not. However, you should strive for a positive thinking score between +1 and +2 for optimal results. Such scores will tend to indicate a level of positive thinking that is not excessively positive to the point that your thoughts are unrealistic or unfounded. At the same time, they will be strong enough to promote self-confidence, self-esteem, and positive interactions with others.

As with other applications of the QCP, the measurement step is important because it provides you with a snapshot of your current thinking patterns, and it offers a means by which you can assess progress later. Thus, this step is inherently linked to the analysis step as well as the revaluation phase of the Quality Core Process. Once you have defined your level of positive thinking (through Fredrickson's positivity ratio or the above positive-negative rating formula), you will have a baseline from which to further evaluate reasons to change your thinking behaviors and strategies.

Step 3 – Why Do You Think the Way You Do?

When I consider the thoughts that I might have at any particular moment, I have noticed they tend to be greatly affected by my perspective and perception at the time. For example, I have taken many examinations in school, as I am sure you have also. Sometimes, when

I was about to take a test, I felt confident and had positive expectations and thoughts about my performance. But in others (perhaps most), I was not as confident, and my thinking tended to be more negative. What was the difference? The key difference was my perception of how well I was prepared and the perspective I had regarding the exam and its level of difficulty. Thus, my thoughts were influenced by both past experiences and future expectations.

Let's take the category of past experiences first. If you have consistently succeeded in the past with little failure, then your level of confidence and self-esteem are likely to be high moving forward. As a result, you will likely maintain a positive outlook about subsequent tasks. In regard to school examinations, experience taught me that my level of performance was linked to how much I studied, how well I knew the material, and my inherent ability to take tests. Each of us has our own set of experiences, and these experiences affect how we view our future endeavors and our abilities. Our past experiences affect whether our thoughts may be more positive or negative moving forward.

At the same time, we use our experiences as well as our knowledge to predict outcomes in the future. I may have enjoyed many positive outcomes in the past, but if I know a future event is different in some way, I will use what knowledge I have to predict the outcome. For example, maybe I have been told a new teacher is incredibly unfair and gives extremely difficult tests. Even if I have performed well on prior exams, this information could trigger negative thinking about future expectations. In essence, your perceptions are based on your existing knowledge, and this affects how you think as well.

Past experiences and future expectations based on knowledge are powerful thought drivers. But as you might suspect, they are not the only ones. Have you ever had the blues and found yourself drowning in negative thoughts? Or maybe you were feeling so wonderful, nothing could stop positive thoughts from running through your mind. Your emotions and how you feel also influence your thoughts. In fact, emotions and thoughts have a reciprocal type of relationship. If you are feeling happy, you are more likely to have positive thoughts. And if you invest in positive thinking, you can improve your mood. Thus, understanding how you feel (and why) can provide insights into why you are thinking the way you do.

So far, we have considered causes of our positive or negative thinking from an internal point of view. In other words, how you interpret your past experiences, perceive the future based on knowledge, and feel emotionally can affect how you think. But you are also affected by things in your environment. Have you ever been around someone who is constantly negative and pessimistic? No matter what subject is being discussed, the conversation always seems to take a negative turn. These individuals remind me of the character on

NBC's *Saturday Night Live*, Debbie Downer.[33] Even in the happiest of times, she constantly sees the worst of things, and in the process drags everyone else down with her. Even the most positive person can be affected by people who are constantly negative.

For any given situation, your past experiences, your current knowledge, your emotional state, and various outside influences combine to affect your thoughts. As a result, when you are examining your positivity ratio or positive-negative ratings of your thoughts, exploring these areas can help you analyze the causes of any negative thinking and identify areas where you can improve your thinking patterns. This analysis will naturally help you select which strategies might provide a higher-quality life from a thought perspective.

The following questions can help you analyze your current level of positive thinking. Use these for particular instances where your thoughts are consumed with a serious issue, or in a more general way to improve your day-to-day thinking patterns.

<u>What past experiences affect how I see things currently (general or specific)?</u>

- Is my view of these past experiences accurate?
- How can I change how I perceive past experiences in a positive way?

<u>What do I expect to happen in the future (general or specific)?</u>

---

33 Saturday Night Live, "Debbie Downer," NBC.com, 2005, http://www.nbc.com/saturday-night-live/video/debbie-downer/3505987?snl=1.

- Are these expectations realistic?
- What information and knowledge support these expectations?
- Is there additional knowledge and information that might change these expectations?

How are my mood and feelings affecting my thoughts (general or specific)?

- Is something triggering my mood to be negative or less positive?
- Am I tired, fatigued, or in pain?

What outside influences affect how I think about things (general or specific)?

- Am I surrounded by positive or negative people?
- Am I involved in positive or destructive activities?
- Can I view my surroundings from a different point of view?

These questions will help you analyze specific areas where you can improve your thinking patterns in an effort to be more positive. You can then select specific strategies in Step 4 to align with the main sources of your negative thoughts while also promoting more positive thinking. While the goal is to become more positive overall, it is not to eliminate all negative thoughts or to become unrealistic in your expectations. Instead, you should strive to achieve more positive than negative perspectives on a daily basis while embracing a healthy level of optimism. This will provide you with the greatest opportunity to improve your quality of life overall.

Step 4 – Strategies to Enhance Positive Thinking

When you think about choosing strategies for promoting positive thought, consider the law of attraction. In essence, positive thoughts facilitate positive thinking, while negative ones attract negative thinking. How many times have you been walking down the street or through the office feeling apathetic when you come across several people smiling? Suddenly you find yourself in a better mood, and everything shifts for the better. Now take the same scenario and imagine everyone you pass has a frown or is showing various levels of frustration. Your reaction is probably not going to be as positive.

Once you start employing various strategies for positive thinking, you will find they become easier over time simply because your positive thoughts encourage continued positive thinking. This is not to say that you will never experience challenges in this regard. Some unforeseen trigger may take you down the path of negative thoughts, leading to negative feelings and greater challenges in your positive thinking efforts. A level of commitment and dedication to thinking positive thoughts will help you maintain positivity in the pursuit of a higher-quality life.

Experiences, knowledge, emotions, and outside influences all combine to have some effect on the thoughts you think. Following are a number of strategies to use to promote positive thinking.

1. Enhance Positive Experiences

- <u>Seek opportunities for positive feedback</u> – In many cases, people do wonderful jobs and fulfill their responsibilities in a superb fashion, but one thing may be lacking . . . feedback. Negative feedback comes easy because everyone is under pressure to perform, meet deadlines, and finish projects. Positive feedback, however, might be an afterthought. In this regard, seek out feedback for your successes. This will encourage others to highlight what you have done well while also giving them a chance to give constructive encouragement in areas needing improvement. These feedback opportunities help create a positive image of yourself, and they help foster positive thinking.

- <u>Invest in activities where self-confidence is high</u> – If you seem to continuously hit roadblocks and setbacks in your endeavors, a repeated sense of failure or poor accomplishment can begin to wear you down. This can naturally lead to less positive thinking as you begin to assume the pattern will occur over and over again. Choose some activities where your chances of success are high. If you're athletic, participate in a community sports league. If you're talented in needlepoint, join a group or sell some of your creative designs at the local craft market. We all need positive experiences, and these fuel our abilities to think positively.

2. Enhance Knowledge and Awareness

- <u>Invest in great preparation</u> – Because your expectations of success and accomplishment can improve with greater levels of preparation, investing in activities that increase your preparedness can lead to increased positive thinking. This is a self-fulfilling prophecy. The more prepared you are, the higher your chances for success. The higher degrees of success you achieve, the more positive you become. And the more positive you become, the more willing you are to prepare for the next challenge.

- <u>Identify how expectations can be shifted</u> – Sometimes it is simply a matter of having unrealistic expectations or a lack of information about the most likely outcome. In these instances, identify what you expect will happen and why. Then, do some investigation and research to determine why you think this is the case. Once you identify the reasons, determine how the situation might be changed to arrive at an outcome that is personally more desirable. Educating yourself about the specifics can be empowering, and focusing on the desired objective promotes a positive environment for thought.

3. Enhance Emotional Well-being

- <u>Perform positive affirmations</u> – Many positivity programs focus on repeating positive affirmations to yourself on a daily basis. Why? Because they work! Surrounding yourself with words of encouragement, happy thoughts, self-empowering statements, and optimism all enhance our emotional well-being. And when we feel positive and good about ourselves, positive thoughts tend to follow.

- <u>Eliminate habits that undermine good feelings</u> – You may have some habits that can lead to negative thinking (or at least weaken positive thoughts about yourself). Sometimes, a lack of exercise, a poor diet, smoking tobacco, or excessive alcohol use might represent habits that lead to negative thinking. Or maybe habits that are incongruent with your beliefs and values are the problem. Try to identify the activities you do that trigger guilt and then determine the source of that guilt. Perhaps the guilt is poorly founded, or maybe you should avoid certain activities. Either way, this can help you improve your ability to think positively.

- <u>Participate in activities that promote emotional (and spiritual) well</u>-being – For me, meditation provides an inner sense of peace that helps promote positive thought. It helps eliminate stress (that can trigger negative thinking) and provides me with a clarity of thought that allows me to better identify sources of positivity and negativity in my life. If a specific activity awards

you these same benefits, then it will also promote positive
thinking to a greater degree in your life.

4. Create a Positive Environment

- <u>Distance yourself from negative situations and people</u> – This
  task can be challenging, especially if you are closely involved
  with a person who is a strongly negative influence or in a
  situation at work where negativity abounds. The goal here
  is to first identify the person or situation and then determine
  how the situation or interaction might be changed. Sometimes,
  confronting the situation or person might be ideal. At other
  times, avoidance maybe necessary. And in both instances, you
  must focus on the one thing you can control . . . your reaction
  to that person and that situation. Putting a positive spin on
  some negative influences can often help keep you thinking
  positive thoughts.

- <u>Seek activities, readings, and individuals that motivate and
  inspire</u> – Just as you will want to minimize and avoid negative
  people and situations, you will also want to surround yourself
  with positive influences. Seek out activities and people who
  energize you, inspire you, motivate you, and encourage you.
  Positive energy is contagious, and being in such an atmosphere
  can tremendously help foster positive thinking.

Step 5 – Periodic Reassessments of Positive Thinking

You have now defined positive thinking (as well as negative thinking), measured your current positivity ratios and positive-negative rankings, analyzed the source of your thinking behaviors, and developed strategies to move toward a higher level of positivity. All that is left is to implement these strategies and determine their effect.

The best way to perform reassessments of your thinking behaviors is to simply repeat your positivity measurements. If your strategies are working (and you are acting on these strategies), then your ratio and your rankings will move toward greater positivity. And if not, then you will need to reanalyze and develop new strategies.

Determining the timing of your reassessments is up to you. However, allowing your strategies time to work is important because reassessments made too quickly or too often may provide inaccurate results. For example, if you need to distance yourself from someone negative in your life, this could take time. Or if you need to replace some unwanted habits with some new ones, reassessments might need to be delayed several months in order to provide a better analysis of your progress. Whatever time period you choose is fine, but make sure you do reassess at some point. The QCP requires periodic reassessments in order to effectively and continually direct you to a more quality-focused life.

In this chapter, you have learned how to apply the QCP to your thinking behaviors so you can enjoy greater positivity and less negativity in your life. More positive thinking can typically lead to a higher-quality life in your mental health, physical health, career, and relationships. At the same time, excessive positivity without consideration for realistic, practical issues can also lead to reduced quality of life. The QCP, therefore, seeks to enhance positive thinking to a degree that allows self-confidence, empowerment, and realistic optimism. With these goals attained, you will enjoy enhanced quality on a daily basis since positive thinking is intimately linked with many other aspects of your life.

Conclusion

"Quality is more important than quantity. One home run is much better than two doubles." – Steve Jobs

As Americans, we are driven to excel. We proudly adopt a hard work ethic, seek to achieve our goals and aspirations, and hope to harvest success from our investments and labor. But sometimes, along the way, we lose track of the things that are critically important to us. We get so wrapped up in our responsibilities and the quantity of tasks at hand that we forget about quality. When this happens, we enjoy less success in life than we might otherwise. For this reason, it is essential that we focus on quality in our endeavors and in every aspect of our lives. In this regard, the quote by Steve Jobs is extremely accurate.

A focus on quality does not mean you have to succeed the first time. Spending too much time thinking about how to "get it right" can cause you to miss out on some great learning and growth experiences. While quality is our goal, never be afraid to try and fail. In this respect, quantity is important also because these trials permit us to better understand the things we do and do not want in our lives, and they show us how best to attain a more desirable environment in which to live. The QCP respects both of these traits. It continually focuses on higher quality, but through a repetitive DMASR cycle, it allows trial and error to help lead the way.

In this book, I have outlined the Quality Core Process. We have applied it in a general way to help guide your life in a more global and comprehensive way, and we have applied the process to specific areas of your life where quality is commonly essential. The QCP is straightforward, simple, and practical. It is also adaptable and can be used to enhance quality in any area of your life. Use the QCP steps (define, measure, analyze, strategize, and reevaluate), alone with dedication and commitment, to attain a higher quality in any area of life you desire.

Now that you have some idea of how to apply the QCP to your personal life, where should you begin? You can certainly start any-where you like since only you can determine where quality is most needed. But as a general rule, applying the QCP in a more general way will greatly help you get the ball rolling. Identify your values, create your own mission statement, your vision statement, and assess gaps in your life where you'd like to enhance quality. Develop some broad strategies upon which you can rely in any situation, and then take another inventory periodically to see where you are. In addition to helping you get familiar with the QCP overall, it will also provide you with a framework to apply to more specific areas of your life later. And such a general approach forces you to take a good look at the things in life that define quality overall.

Next, tackle the more problematic aspects where quality is lacking in your life. Do you lack quality in your career or your relationships? Perhaps you are unhappy with how well you are managing your finances or your health. Regardless of the issues you identify, whether ones in this book or others, the QCP will help you move in a direction of higher quality. The process has been proven to be effective time and time again in business, and I can attest it is equally effective as a quality-promoting tool in your personal life as well. All it takes is a few committed steps, and you will be well on your way to a better and more fulfilling life.

Each aspect of your life, from your career to your personal relationships, is deeply interconnected. A chain is only as strong as its weakest link, so it is critical to apply the QCP to every piece of your life. Let's briefly recap the steps in achieving personal quality control in your life.

- Quality Control over your career: What is your dream job, and what will it take for you to move to this position? Assess the skills you need for this job and the barriers in your way and . . . take action.
- Quality Control over your health: What are your health goals? How do you intend to reach these goals, and what's the biggest

obstacle standing in your way? Make a plan and execute, but don't be too hard on yourself. Nothing great comes easily, and living a healthy life takes hard work and time. Remember to invest in yourself above everything else.

- <u>Quality Control over your finances:</u> Assess your spending habits and consider where your money actually goes. Track your spending for each month and evaluate your habits. The first step in getting help is recognizing you have a problem. Saving isn't easy for anyone, but by dedicating time to financial planning you will be more likely to identify exactly why you're not where you'd like to be. Make a realistic plan each month and make lifestyle changes.

- <u>Quality Control over your relationships:</u> What do you value most in your relationships? Identify the people in your life who either drain or empower you, and pursue only those relationships that benefit you.

- <u>Quality Control over your thinking:</u> What is the right attitude for success in life? Positivity and hope are what fuel ambition and accomplishment. Inventory your thoughts and develop a strategy to enhance positive thinking.

While this book serves as an excellent resource and guide in applying the QCP to your life, other resources and tools are available to you as well. Specifically, QCP workshops and seminars are available for individuals and businesses alike. Likewise, workbooks are also available to assist you with specific steps of the QCP in many life areas. These instruments and aids can help you get started, and in time, you will become more adept at applying the Quality Core Process. Each time you repeat the DMASR cycle, it will become more and more intuitive. This is how quality can continually build upon itself as you progress in your efforts.

As a quality control expert and one who is dedicated to helping others succeed, my hope is for you to effectively apply the QCP in your own life. We all want quality in every area of our lives, and its pursuit makes us better both individually and collectively. Unfortunately, we sometimes miss the forest for the trees at times (or vice versa), and our pursuits may take us off the path we would like to follow. The QCP provides the means to get us back on track. In doing so, you can have the quality life you desire while making a positive impact on those around you at the same time.

About The Author

Ryan Greene is an entrepreneur, speaker, and author of the book: *Quality Controlled – Personal Fulfillment Through Professional Organization*. He lives in Rock Springs, WY with his wife Lindsey, his son Karsen and daughter Kynlee. He is an avid reader, loves the outdoors and is a repeat spelling violator.

For the past decade Ryan has been a Quality Control Specialist within his family's oil and gas service company. Utilizing QC programs such as Six Sigma, The 5P's, Total Quality Management, and Strategic Quality Management has allowed Ryan to developed his own Quality Control System. The Quality Core Process (QCP) brings the same techniques and strategies of pursuing quality in the corporate world and makes them personal. Everyone can enjoy a greater quality of life utilizing Ryan's QCP process.

Over the past seven years Ryan has spoken to thousands of people all over the world sharing principles in leadership, quality control, management techniques and even a recent 2016 US Congressional Campaign (which was unsuccessful, but that's a different story).

Ryan's Personal Mission Statement – "To achieve ever-increasing knowledge to empower others."

Ryan's Personal Vision Statement – "To empower every person to pursue a high-quality life through deeper personal understanding."

www.ingramcontent.com/pod-product-compliance
Lightning Source LLC
Chambersburg PA
CBHW052006090426
42741CB00008B/1567